Teaching French

Teaching French

R. J. Hares

HODDER AND STOUGHTON
LONDON SYDNEY AUCKLAND TORONTO

In memory of my father
and to the French teachers
of Carlisle participating
in In-Service courses 1971–5

British Library Cataloguing in Publication Data
Hares, R J
    Teaching French.
    1. French language – Study and teaching
    I. Title
    440'.7'1   PC2065

ISBN 0 340 23196 3

Copyright © 1979 R. J. Hares

All rights reserved. No part of this publication may be
reproduced or transmitted in any form or by any means,
electronic or mechanical, including photocopy, recording,
or any information storage and retrieval system, without
permission in writing from the publisher.

Set, printed and bound in Great Britain for
Hodder and Stoughton Educational
a division of Hodder and Stoughton Ltd.,
Mill Road, Dunton Green, Sevenoaks, Kent,
by Cox and Wyman Ltd, London, Fakenham and Reading

Contents

Preface xi
1 Group Work: Theory and Practice 1

Advantages of group work 1
What is group work? 2
Teacher control 3
Controlled group work 3
Free group work 4
A detailed example of course book adaptation:
The teacher-based introduction, 4; Initial teacher-based practice, 5; The first group practice, 6; The demonstration group, 6; The controlled group rehearsal, 7; The individual group practice, 7; The work cards 8.
Range of group-based activities 8
The basic course outline 9
Difficult structures 9
Difficult individuals 10
Comprehension work 10
Reading 11
Writing 11
Conversations: Minute conversations, 12; Teacher stimulus, 13; Conversation control cards, 13; Controlled practice, 13; Structure practice, 14; The 'dare' element, 14; Monitoring and language error, 14; The totally oral lesson, 15; Noise, 15.

2 Mixed Ability Teaching 17

Independent group work, 17; Flexible French 18.
Responsibility for assessment 18
The top band 19

vi TEACHING FRENCH

 The middle band   19
 Single skill testing   20
 Teacher movement   21
 The group lesson cycle   21
 The lower band, 23; The problem of
 concentration, 23; Top group help, 24.

3 Group Activities   25

 Oral techniques, 25; Peer situations, 25; The
 interrogative; 26;
 **Basic question and answer routine (Teacher
 controlled)** 26: Familiarity of material, 27.
 Sample work cards: *C'est toi le coupable*
 (Descriptive discovery), 27; *Sur le plan* (Map
 description), 29; *Faites bien attention,* 31; *On
 recherche,* 32; *Non!* 32; *Les huiles!* 32; Cloze activities,
 33; *A la fin,* 34; *Qu'est-ce que je dois dire?* 35; *Quelque
 chose qui commence par* ... 35.
 Early sentence recognition and copy writing,
 35; *Trouvez la phrase,* 36; *A la fin,* 36; *Racontez nous
 l'histoire,* 36.
 Initiative activities, 36; *Grosse tête,* 37; *Les mots
 croisés,* 37; Competition, 38; *Déchiffrez-lé-moi,* 39.
 Early reading strategies, 39; Silent reading, 39;
 Reading aloud, 40; *Ecouté-moi,* 40.
 Tape recorder activities, 40: Gist reading, 40;
 Au secours, 40; *Communications téléphoniques,* 41.
 The slide viewer, 41; Vocabulary recognition,
 42; *Ce qui commence par* ... 42;
 Story composition, 42.
 Oral activities (card guided), 42.

4 The Work Card Concept   44

 Card grading   44
 Memory tests   45
 The basic card   46
 Card coding   46
 Longevity   46
 Pupil production of cards   47
 Work cards for the early stages   47
 The early tape recorder card   49
 Jigsaw sentences   49
 Slide cards   50

Initiative work 51
The map work card 51
Graded work cards for the Longman's
adaptation: *A l'ordre* (Disguised copy-writing), 53;
Qu'est-ce qui manque? (Fill in the missing words),
54; *Rafraichissez-moi là mémoire* (Sound and written
shape recall), 54; *Entre toi et moi* (Paired
dictations), 55; Substitution-translation card, 55.

5 Work Card Activities 56

Filmstrip work cards, 56; Filtrage (screen test),
57; Card adaptation, 57; *Vérifiez-le!* 57; *Ça finit
comment?* 58; *Écrivez la fin vous-même!* 58; *Truquage!*
59; Typical difficulties, 60.
Overhead projector work cards, 60; *C'est quoi la
silhouette?* 60; *Pour aller ..?* 61; *Ce n'est plus là!* 62;
Avant 62.
Radio broadcasts, 62; Basic assignments, 63;
Réponses rapides (French short answer techniques),
64; *Radio Nous!* (Exploded text), 64; *Faites votre
choix* (Multiple choice), 65; Categories 66.
Language laboratory work cards, 67;
Conversation téléphonique (Paired link-ups), 68;
Dialogue (role playing), 68; *Faites le commentaire*
(Filmstrip commentaries), 68; *Les voix des gens*
(limitations), 70;
**Practical, job-centred and general interest
cards,** The Car Card, 72; The Cookery Card, 72;
The Fashion Card, 73; The Commerce Card, 74;
The Football Card, 75.

6 The Preparation and Use of Visual and Taped Materials 76

Basic picture and flash cards, 76; Picture
source, 76; Adhesives, 76; Professional
finish, 77; Highlighting, 77; Contour bordering,
77; Labelling, 77; Captions, 77; Picture
transposition, 77; Humour, 78.
Photographs, 78; Selection of detail, 78;
Photographic slides, 78; Supplementing the
course book, 79.
Overhead projector materials, 79; Flexibility,
79; Advantages, 79; Long-term storage, 79;

Overlay transparencies, 80.
Offset-copier visuals, 80; Worksheets, 80.
Projector prints, 80.
Taped materials, 81; Recording conditions, 81; Leader Tapes, 81; Coding system; Splicing, 82; Renovation of material, 82; Splicing in, 82; Teacher and assistant-made tapes, 82; Direct microphone recordings (recording speeds, speed of utterance, repetition gaps, voice composition, voice variation, microphone sound effects, signature tunes), 82–83; Cassettes, 83.

7 General Classroom and Lesson Procedure   85

Classroom instruction in French, 85; A phased introduction of commands, 86; The register in French, 87.
Class routine and pupil involvement, 88; Specific responsibilities, 88; Pupil operatives, 88; The pupil rota, 89; The weekly rota, 90; Numbering and cataloguing, 90; Class control, 91.
Difficult schools and children, 91; An alternative curriculum, 92; Practical and job-centred activities, 92; Certificates of achievement, 93; Survival situations, 93; CSE Modes II and III 93.

8 Classroom Display and Decoration   94

Starting from nothing   94
Pupil participation   94
The classroom division, 95; Clearly separate sections, 95; Logical ordering, 95; Detachability of material, 96; The L-shaped structure, 96; A touch of class, 96; The class mascot, 96; The ceiling discovered, 96; Ringing the changes, 97.
Activity areas and interest corners   98
The geography corner, 98; The basic map, 98; Display arrows, 99; Wool arrows, 99; *Cherchez l'erreur,* 99; *Cherchez l'intrus,* 99; Number, distance and kilometre work, 100; The arrowed picture, 100; Clutter, 100; The photo/picture display, 100; Small displays, 101.
The grammar corner, 101; Figurines, 101;

Meaning by picture, 102; Coded question marks, 102; The 'où' question mark, 102; The visual equation, 103; Logical relationships, 103; Sentence cards, 103; balloon sentences, 104; Colour coding, 104; Split sentences, 104.
The vocabulary corner, 105; Extra vocabulary, 105; Vertical course material, 106; The teacher's limited French vocabulary, 106; Vocabulary grouping, 107; Relation pairing, 107; Rhyming pairs and groups 107.

The prop and costume store   108
The post box   108

Further reading   109

Useful addresses   110

Index   111

The author acknowledges use of the Schools Council Project Concepts 7–9 as a basis for *C'est toi le coupable!* and *Sur le plan*, with thanks.

Preface

The manual is a drawing together of years of work with practising teachers of French and with student teachers. It does not set out to be comprehensive. Neither could it be without running to several thousands of pages, but it does try to provide strategies and practical suggestions that work, and that make the teaching of French an easier and more enjoyable job than it often is.

Inevitably, in a work of this kind, there is a considerable overlap between chapters, though the manual has been designed to help the teacher select specific strategies and activities which will be of use in the classroom. In this connexion, I would be very pleased to hear from those of you with amendments or refinements to the techniques suggested, as the many excellent ideas you must have would be welcome to colleagues everywhere.

Thanks are due to fellow teachers and generations of students and pupils for the impetus they have provided. Special thanks to Anthony Barley, Mike Buckby, Michael Chislett, John Daniels, Susan Day, Geneviève Elliott, Tom Ferguson, John Green, Jane Hetherington, Peter Kearle, Peter Lavin, David Nott, Bill Price, Eric Richardson, Bill Romanis, Robin Sanderson, Peter Squibb, Richmond Turner, Peter Walker, Roy Walls, David Westgate, Norman White and the late Norman Shave for their help and encouragement.

R. J. H.
Northumberland College of
Higher Education,
Ponteland,
Newcastle upon Tyne

Chapter 1

Group Work: Theory and Practice

Group work is the concept offered as a panacea to teachers everywhere who find difficulty in teaching modern languages to all but advanced students, yet the amount of group work used remains quite small. The average teacher feels he or she would like to use it, but does not do so in practice. Whatever the reasons given for not attempting a group work approach to French, they tend to distil down into uncertainty, not really as to the merits of the method, but as to its practical application. It is not so much a matter of why?, but how, specifically? The question is a valid one. To change from a teacher-based, front-of-the-class approach to that of groups working independently, with the teacher taking on a monitoring and servicing role for a large part of the lesson is a mammoth change. Such changes in classroom technique do not just happen; they have to be planned. For such planning, class teachers need help, not because they are incapable of doing the job themselves, but because they have a full-time, stressful job and it is unrealistic to expect the professional teacher to cope with the continuous demands and frustrations of the day, take home marking, prepare lessons and teaching aids and find the time and energy to conceive a whole new working strategy. It is with such a situation in mind that the suggestions below are offered.

If a look is taken at some of the justifications often quoted for the use of group work in French lessons and it is found that at least a few of them are relevant to the problems inherent in one's own particular teaching situation, then it is worth giving serious thought to the group work approach. Such an approach can facilitate:

a The division of the class into satisfactory random, social, or ability groups.
b The exploitation and cementing of newly acquired language material.
c The introduction of a more child-centred or pupil-based method.
d Greater harmony with the integrated-day concept.

e The adaptation of blanket-cover commercial courses to the differing needs, abilities and levels within the class.
f General interest and project work.
g The introduction of reading.
h The introduction of writing.
i The productive use of any left-over time.
j The easing of the strain on the teacher.

Group work can achieve all or none of these aims, depending on how it is implemented, yet asked to choose which single aim out of the above list was the most vital, one might well select the last; not merely out of professional sympathy with colleagues straining to meet the considerable physical demands of teacher-based oral lesson after teacher-based oral lesson, but also for the soundly logical reason that a less strained teacher is likely to function better in most areas of his work, to everyone's benefit.

Before discussing a practical plan of campaign directed towards achieving these aims, let us consider some perfectly understandable objections to what would seem to be group work. Most teachers will know someone who has tried a little such work, with possibly unpleasant results for himself and for next door. Objections will take something of the form of *They're a noisy class, you know, at the best of times, and have to be kept under control. You can't have them working in groups on their own. That's why Mrs. Stokoe had trouble when she tried it!*

If, on the evidence of noise from next door and others' stated loss of control, we are determined that group work is a non-starter, then it will be very difficult to argue the opposing case. However, if we are dissatisfied with the way our French teaching is proceeding, it is arguably worth trying, particularly if we could admit the possibility that the hypothetical Mrs. Stokoe was trying something very different from a carefully thought-out group work plan and that the concept of group work has a variety of interpretations, many of which might seem to be rather hazy.

What, then, is group work? Group work properly conceived, that is. It is not running dry seven minutes from the end of a lesson, dividing the class into arbitrary groups and telling them to start talking about anything in French. It is not having one group practising a dramatic and loud dialogue, while the rest are supposed to be quietly reading or writing. It is not dividing the class into groups and getting them to repeat after the tape recorder for a quarter of an hour, followed by the rest of a teacher-based, front-delivered lesson, the children still sitting in groups but doing nothing differently from an ordinary lesson.

It is a system in which children, divided into groups on whatever basis the teacher sees fit, can work at pair, group or single activities within their group, or indeed in conjunction with another group. A statement like the last allows for so much that it risks saying nothing, but it should indicate *a* that the teacher can please himself as to the specific line taken within a fairly broad spectrum, *b* that there is a considerable amount of room for variation and for ringing the changes within the lesson. But one is still not being very specific, particularly if the intention is to look for something to plan that will not fall to pieces for lack of a deliberate method. Whatever activities the teacher might think of adapting to group work, whichever groups he can see himself using it with, refinements and shades of application are best left for the moment to allow a precise look at what might be done to introduce a group work pattern into the lesson.

When planning method, one should start by dispelling the illusion that the teacher cedes control to the pupils. Ideally, in a well-run class, it may look like this to the observer from outside, but control is not lost. It is merely less obtrusive and starts with a planned disposition of the chairs, desks and tables. Whatever the basis on which groups are selected, the class is arranged so that the teacher has ease of access to each group, if at all practicable. Children whose behaviour is likely to be difficult or disruptive are sat where they are particularly attainable, in those areas of the room we have the best view of and/or in which one is likely to do the most walking, notwithstanding a general policy of possibly equal attention for all the groups.

The way is now open to consider the running of the lesson itself, from the point of view of what the teacher does and omitting for the moment the question of materials, group composition, etc.

Assuming that materials have been prepared (see Chapters 3–6) and the groupings thought out, the teacher has the option of adopting a partial or 'full' commitment to a group-work approach. 'Full' stands in inverted commas, since the term 'full group work approach' is at least partially misleading. One may use group-work for ten minutes from time to time, as part of a lesson, or as the basic technique for the majority of one's teaching programme. But, even with this 'full' commitment, there must still be a degree of teacher-based activity, to introduce and exploit grammatical points, structures, comprehensions, paradigms, dialogues—in fact, the essential language activities. With this realisation in mind and working from the tried and tested teaching principle that abrupt change from one method to another with no attempts at transition will usually lead to chaos, the technique is introduced, employing a pattern of what may be termed 'controlled' and 'free group-work'—in that order.

Controlled group work is a successful way of guiding the class into group work, through parts of a teacher-based method which are recognisable and accepted by the children. It starts, inevitably, with the teacher introducing the material, whether it is new structure or lexis, or a practice or exploitation activity related to something with which the children are already at least partly familiar. After the teacher introduction to all the class, the work in groups begins. The pattern of controlled group work activity would run:

    a *Teacher-based introduction.*
    b *First group practice* for all groups, with the teacher controlling from base and personally involved.
    c *A demonstration group*, i.e. one of the set groups, or a mixture from all the groups, working or acting out the activity just practised, for all the rest of the class to see and hear.
    d *Controlled group rehearsal*, which differs from *b* in that the teacher is not now actively involved, but controls the pace from base.

From here, the teacher moves on to free group work for *e* and *f* to complete the pattern:

    e *Individual group practice*, which is a natural extension of *d*, with the children working through the activity at their own speed and the teacher circulating and monitoring.
    f *Work cards*—picture recognition and various drawing, painting, reading and written activities, based on the material just or recently practised and graded to suit the different groups within the class.

The attraction of such a method is that it does enable both pupil and teacher to acclimatise to a new system, because it is a series of logical steps and incorporates much with which both teacher and taught are already familiar. At the same time, however, the term 'work cards' implies additional preparation. If this is impossible, then not all will be lost by discarding *f* from the pattern. For many colleagues, group work hinges on work card activities and Chapter 4 should help to show how work cards may be produced *en masse*, without the class teacher having to be the sole manufacturer.

For those dedicated to a technique broadly similar to the one above, it may, indeed, have its beauty, but for people not too familiar with the system, practical examples are called for, so one can see exactly what is implied by the categories *a–f* in specific situations.

The example given is a slightly adapted dialogue from Unit 2 of Longman's Audio-Visual French, Stage 2, used with a set of twelve to thirteen year olds. The adapted dialogue differs from the original only in the addition of one sentence and one new character, who appropriates certain utterances previously accredited to one of the original five characters. This latter change occurs to fit the dialogue to groups of six.

A Group-Work Adaptation

Stage a. The Teacher-Based Introduction.
From his or her normal teaching base, the teacher familiarises the class

Michel	Eh bien, messieurs-dames. Qu'est-ce que vous prenez?
Claudette	Moi, je prends une glace au chocolat.
Jean-Paul	Et moi, je prends une limonade.
Pierre	Hélène et moi, nous prenons un chocolat glacé.
Claude	Moi, je prends un citron pressé.
Jean-Paul	Michel, veux-tu prendre quelque chose avec nous?
Michel	Merci mon vieux, mais je ne prends rien quand je travaille.
Hélène	Tu as beaucoup de clients.
Claude	Il n'y a plus de tables libres.
Michel	Oui, quand il fait beau beaucoup de gens prennent une glace.
Claudette	Jean-Paul, prends ce panier.
Jean-Paul	Je le mets à côté de ma chaise.
Pierre	Attention, ne le mets pas là.
Claude	Michel ne va pas le voir.
Hélène	Mettons-le sous la table. Mais ne l'oublie pas.
Michel	Voilà, messieurs-dames. Une glace au chocolat et une limonade.
Claudette	Je les prends.
Hélène	Voilà ta limonade, Jean-Paul.
Michel	Pierre, veux-tu prendre les chocolats?
Pierre	Oui, je les ai.
Claude	Toi, tu vas les payer, Hélène, n'est-ce pas?

Fig. 1 The adapted dialogue

with the dialogue material in the normal way, by linking film-strip and tape and eliciting questions and answers during the previous lesson(s). Depending on whether or not the children are to commit their parts to memory, they are given their roles either the lesson before or at the beginning of the actual group-dialogue lesson. As the children will normally be sitting in their groups anyway, and to avoid chaos during the allocation of roles, a simple procedure may be adopted to save time, temper and tantrum. The teacher gives each character in the dialogue a number and then has a set of cards with the requisite numbers distributed to each group. Each pupil takes a card, with the proviso that certain numbers are for the boys in the group, others for the girls, and one number (corresponding to *Claude*) for either a boy or girl, to avoid possible gender-shock. If, for some reason, there are not six people in the group, then the additional role can be discarded.

The group work lesson begins with a straightforward practice-repetition of the taped dialogue, with the teacher adding the one extra sentence at the appropriate point. Most recent evidence and particularly the NFER report *Primary French in the Balance* warns of the hostility to chorus repetition of taped material, and understandably. Here, though, one faces quite a different situation from the usual classroom chorus. The fact that the children know they are going to act out the dialogue for

Fig. 2 The picture sheet for the adapted dialogue. (From page 18 of Longman's Audio-Visual French Stage 2, by kind permission of the publisher.)

themselves in their own groups, with the help of a fairly comprehensive prop store and clothes brought in for the occasion, establishes something of a different perspective on *Répétez, tout le monde! Répétition*, here, takes on something of its meaning in the theatre. After perhaps two runs through the repetition, the class may be ready for:

Stage b. The First Group Practice.
For this practice the pupils may or may not have a copy of the text of the dialogue, depending on *i* the teacher's intentions, *ii* the ability of the class, *iii* the needs of specific groups within the class. So, the situation exists where all, some, or none of the children might have their copy.

This run-through is controlled completely and directly by the teacher, who indicates the speaker from a list of the *personnae* on the board, reads out the line and has every *Hélène* or *Jean-Paul* practise their line. At all stages up to and including Stage *d*, the children might practise with or without their copy of the text in front of them.

Stage c. The Demonstration Group.
The demonstration group is nothing more than the name implies, as indicated on page 4, but if the groups have been situated so that there is

something of a natural stage area, it will allow the audience to form a clear picture of what they are going to do when it is their turn.

The teacher allows the volunteer or chosen group to work through the dialogue with some prompting and perhaps a little example interpretation from him or her, and then proceeds to:

Stage d. The Controlled Group Rehearsal.
Although this is a group rehearsal and the teacher is not actively involved in the dialogue, he nonetheless has complete and direct control of this run-through. This is achieved by the teacher calling out or pointing in turn to the name (on the board) of the next speaker in the dialogue.

Such a technique, though appearing Pavlovian, allows every *Pierre* or *Claudette* to speak at the right time, in relative peace and without being put off by hearing different lines from near at hand. At this stage, with increasing familiarisation with the dialogue as the main consideration, the gestures and actions that will have been practised in the previous stage may be kept at a minimum if so required. Now the class should be gaining some confidence and one may move on to the first of the two free group work stages, namely

Stage e. The Individual Group Practice.
Whatever has happened in Stages *a–d*, the children ought now to work without written material, with the single, important exception of one member of the group who retains the text to act as prompter. Such a duty can have been allocated when the numbers were originally distributed and here one can see the advantage of a numbers system. Most teachers would insist that the job of prompter should go round the group from dialogue to dialogue. Hard as one tries, it is often difficult to remember who did what last time, and having to ask the children when dealing with five or six different groups is likely to produce disputes and noise. A rota will help to avoid disruption and will be seen as fair. With a prompter to provide support, groups are far less likely to grind to a halt—a phenomenon which often ruins so much potentially good group work —and this frees the teacher for the vital task of monitoring.

Such a system will not be perfect to start with, but there is no reason why the machine should not soon become well-oiled. A statement like the last might well be taken as indicative of regimentation. If that impression is given, it is an unfortunate and incorrect one, because once the machine is working and the children know where they are, all sorts of surprising and welcome things start happening. The process is well-ordered so that the children can work constructively and enjoy themselves, and this is so often seen in the excellent character acting and personal involvement that a reasonable class gradually achieves.

Excellent as such dialogues are in themselves, useful as they may be for encouraging self-expression, they are also being utilised to develop the child's general understanding and use of French. Teachers would feel they were doing their pupils a disservice if they did not attempt to cement in some form or other the material over which the pupils gain some control during their dialogue work.

Stage f. Work Cards.
With this latter aim in mind, work cards provide the flexibility for meaningful reinforcement material for a wide range of different abilities and interests within the class (see Chapters 2, 4 and 5) and give balance to and round off the lesson.

The work cards used in the above example lesson are shown and analysed in the chapter on work cards (pages 51–55). They were conceived to produce a series of graded language activities which would keep the class meaningfully and productively occupied. The work card activity had some ten minutes, or a quarter of the lesson, devoted to it, so the particular lesson under examination was a predominantly oral one. With such a group of twelve to thirteen year olds the next lesson could, if it were thought necessary, contain a lengthier written and a reading session to provide a balance for the children. But here again, the point is that a group work method, with work card activities as a major element, ought to be flexible enough for the teacher to alter it as required. The continuous and unrelieved use of the pattern just looked at will eventually have the same effect as any other continuous and unrelieved teaching pattern. Nonetheless, in the early stages of working with the children in groups it is worth adhering to the 'controlled developing into free group work' plan for the children to become gradually accustomed to running part of their own lesson.

Equally gradually, the class can be weaned to the position from where a major part of the lesson can be group controlled. But again we are in need of practical examples, so, as a preliminary, it might be worthwhile analysing some of the activities already undertaken within the lesson during the pupil's first few years of learning French and seeing how such activities can be used to produce a predominantly group-based lesson. Here one thinks of time spent on comprehension work, reading, writing, conversations, commands, quizzes, general games, acting, miming, picture work, art work, project work, word or sentence composition, and the use of the tape recorder or slide viewer.

Teachers of French supplied with a Teacher's Book have had many years of feeling that they must follow someone else's lesson plans almost to the letter, whereas it is up to us to believe sufficiently in ourselves to choose the variety of activity we ourselves would like, provided only it offers a balance which will allow the French to be learned effectively and not encourage, for example, concentration on the oral skills to the virtual exclusion of the others and vice versa. These are fine words, but again there is the need to be practical. A whole gamut of activities has just been listed, but they must have a recognisable base on which to be set. Inevitably, that base must still be the course book. At this point, one uncovers the basic and very understandable fear behind many a teacher's reluctance to adapt material. If the book is not used almost verbatim, will not the children suffer and go to their next school either knowing not enough or the wrong material? A second basic fear is that mistakes of language will be made when the teacher transposes from the publisher's to his own material. A third, no less understandable, apprehension is the feeling the children will not take to the new materials produced. If one follows the basic outline of the course supplied, such consequences can be avoided and planning and organisation made so much easier.

'Following the basic outline' may mean several things, depending on the degree to which the materials supplied suit the class. It is significant that in French more than almost any other subject, the teacher is continually being exhorted to adapt, try this, try that. This, surely, is a clear indication that no one course, as it stands, meets the needs of all the learners in one class. Nor, by the nature of things, can it. Depending, then, on how happy one is with the basic course, the decision will have to be made as to what extent the outline is followed, remembering that the more radical the departure from what has been already prepared, the more work group work adaptation is likely to require. A good compromise point is to follow the list of structures to be learnt (usually outlined in the Teacher's Book) and the basic part of each unit or chapter. If a tacit agreement is made to adhere to the list and the basic lesson material, this is far from conceding that they have to be tackled exactly as suggested in the Teacher's Notes or as printed in the text. Similarly, one may find that certain structures and comprehension material always cause problems at the recommended point of introduction. For example, a teacher may feel that, when it comes to introducing *Combien de ... y a-t-il? Il y en a ...*, the amount of time spent on obtaining *Il y en a huit* rather than *Il y en a huit chevaux* is entirely out of proportion to the value of the structure. If this is the case, he should feel free to decide on a very brief introduction or, alternatively, gradual acquaintanceship. Or again, depending on the group and lesson organisation, he may teach it to his most able children in advance of the main class.

As far as what one might label comprehension material is concerned, there are in most courses units where the narrative, dialogue or episode is misplaced and there are linguistic difficulties far beyond the present competence of the average child in the class. As long as substitute methods can be found for practising the new structure and important vocabulary contained in the unit, there is no reason why misplaced activities should not be put in cold storage or totally removed.

From here, it is a short step to using, for example, the *situations* in *En*

Avant as the basis of the fortnightly unit work and omitting the rest of the material practised in the unit in favour of one's own adaptations. Here, one might find that the workbooks and readers provided by *En Avant* would prove an excellent base material for general adaptation.

Whether the teacher sticks closely or loosely to the base, the disposition of the class into groups of whatever nature will mean several different activities proceeding at the same time. The immediate objections to this are the question of indiscipline and the inordinate amount of time ostensibly required for the preparation of a variety of materials.

Though it will help, the placing of difficult individuals in the positions where they are more strategically available will not solve a basic behaviour problem, but up to middle secondary level a variety of passably interesting and individualised materials and activities will provide further assistance. As a general rule of thumb, if a class is proving difficult, greater control is often achieved by stepping up the amount of written work card based activity. If a boy or girl is proving particularly unamenable, one of the advantages of card work is the fact that it is much easier to find something extra for him or her to do during the lesson and the break time.

From the point of view of materials preparation, the term 'ostensibly' used above is justified. The secret of much effective group work and the saviour of many a teacher's sanity is the decision to use the materials and hardware already available in as many ways as possible. If this is done, preparation time can be cut down appreciably.

Comprehension work

If the teacher looks for straightforward comprehension exercises that can be done without him, he may be surprised by the number of alternatives available. But before examining these, there is the question of preparation time. It is strange how a text lifted from a book can look much more interesting and relevant when stuck on a piece of card and given to an individual child. One just does not have the time to copy out *en bloc* passage after passage to produce an inexhaustible supply of cards for pupils. If on the other hand there are half a dozen books to be thrown away, before doing so one can inspect them, indicate the passages to be cut out and get pupils to cut and paste up—either at home, if they can be relied upon, or as volunteers during a wet weather playtime. The same pupils can then write the instructions on the emerging work card, if the activity is kept simple enough.

Building up a corpus of such activities, one might well start with cards requiring a short, straightforward summary of the passage in English. Or pertinent words, phrases and sentences in the text can be underlined and an explanation required. Alternatively, such items can be blocked out, with the gaps to be filled from a list inserted at the bottom of the card; the passage can be accompanied by a questionnaire in English or in French, to be answered in either language according to the level of the child's competence; the pupil may be asked to extract from the text all those sentences relevant to him or herself or the classroom or the home; or the passage left deliberately incomplete, with the task being to finish the story (once again, in English or in French); for paired work, one pupil may be required to ask questions and the other to answer from the text; the pupil may be given another passage and asked to insert as many sentences as possible from the second into the first, providing they make sense; or missing vocabulary given underneath the passage and the pupil required to insert this lexis in the correct places. (See Fig. 24, page 54.)

Reading

Reading texts obtained in perhaps the same way as suggested in the section on comprehension work are used for silent or loud reading. Using a similar method to initial reading schemes in the mother tongue, each child would have a (not too large) set of passages to work through during the year and would be heard by the teacher as he or she came round to each group. If readers are available with the course, then they would be the basis for such work and would also be used for comprehension work along the lines discussed above.

Silent reading might be practised in a similar way to general library work, with a set number of passages and reading cards to be got through. If it were felt necessary to test silent reading progress then it could be assessed using some of the activities outlined in the section on comprehension work.

Writing

Work card based group activities are a natural vehicle for writing practice at all stages from initial copy-writing to advanced picture composition. There are many basic activities that can be devised. At the earlier levels one can, for example, produce copy exercises containing an element of challenge for the pupil by employing multiple choice techniques. The teacher might produce a card on the theme of 'The Weather' with several small pictures and under each one a gapped sentence for completion, with three possibilities from which to choose, e.g.:

Quand . . . . , je ne sors pas. (il fait beau/il fait du soleil/il pleut)

Or, by way of variation, a double gap, but still related to a specific picture:

$$\left.\begin{array}{l} \textit{En hiver} \\ \textit{Au printemps} \\ \textit{En été} \end{array}\right\} \textit{je vais} \left\{\begin{array}{l} \textit{`a la plage} \\ \textit{dans la montagne} \\ \textit{chez le médecin} \end{array}\right.$$

Other writing activities are dealt with in the chapters on work cards, pages 35–75.

Conversations

Group free conversations are a subject of controversy because of the noise level, the inevitable inaccuracies of unsupervised speech and the obvious opportunity they offer the pupil to sit back and do nothing. All of these are, of course, valid objections. Add to them the fact that a child with a minimum level of French would find it difficult if not impossible to maintain a conversation for anything more than a minute, and one may seem to have succeeded in dismissing such an activity out of hand.

Let us start with the last objection, since it is arguably the most fundamental and not unrelated to the others.

To attempt to obtain lengthy conversations from beginners and near beginners in the language is, we accept, self-defeating. And it is when one attempts this that the noise level really rises. If it is thought that pairs within a group can sustain a conversation of a minute, then there is much to be said for taking the minute as the basic unit. Immediately one realises that getting groups to work on a particular activity for a minute only is certain to be more trouble than it is worth. So an effective solution is produced by giving the pairs five small conversation topics to be covered in five to seven minutes.

How, then, does the teacher service this activity to eliminate chaos and her consort, the broken sound-barrier?—which latter, apart from ruining relationships with neighbouring teachers, makes it impossible to monitor what is going on. Though in such a not-so-hypothetical noisy situation, there will probably be very little French to monitor.

It is stating the obvious to say that paired conversations have to be practised in the control situation before pupils can ever be expected to work on them sensibly on their own. But even this direct statement seems to be begging the question as to how this practice is brought about and what, anyway, constitutes a conversation for beginners or even relative beginners.

A conversation of a minute between two people after only a few months' French is not too demanding once the children become used to what is expected of them. After a short experience of French one might reasonably expect conversations such as:

a *Qu'est-ce que c'est? ... C'est un ballon. ... C'est un ballon bleu? ... Non, il est rouge. ... C'est le ballon de Pierre? ... Oui. ... Non, c'est le ballon de Fred!*
b *Comment t'appelles-tu? ... (Je m'appelle) Belphégor. ... Moi, je m'appelle (je suis) Fernand. ... Quel âge as-tu? ... (J'ai) dix ans, et toi? ... (J'ai) onze ans. ... Tu as un frère? ... Non, (mais j'ai) une sœur. ... Comment s'appelle-t-elle? ... Diana.*
c *Où habites-tu? ... Belsay. ... C'est loin? ... Oui. ... C'est une ville? ... Non, (c'est) un village. ... Tu habites dans un appartement? ... Non, une maison. ... Elle est jolie? ... Oui. Toi, tu as une maison? ... Oui. ... Où? ... À Ponteland.*

Such conversations, which will have developed out of the normal corpus of material covered, will need some stimulus from the teacher if they are to be put together. In the early stages, with the teacher controlling the pairs from his or her normal teaching point, the conversations can be helped along by the use of straightforward visual aids.

For discussion **a**, a card with a neutral-coloured ball and question mark, followed by a blue ball, question mark and a cross, then a red ball plus tick and the names Pierre (with a cross) and Fred (with a tick), will contain all the visual information necessary. But, of course, without practice with the teacher it does not succeed at all, except for those with a high I.Q. The teacher practises every part of the conversation as many times as required with everybody practising all of it and then allocates roles **A** and **B** to the pairs so that at this still early stage each member of the pair knows who is doing what. A conversation when it is first put together may well take up as much as half the lesson, if so required.

When the roles have been gone through under control conditions with the teacher ensuring that the pupils are always at the point they should be, as in the Longman's adaptation (pages 6–7), then the conversation is at its most artificial. But one would probably accept the principle that a basic routine must be learnt before it can be adapted. When the children are beginning to be happy with the dialogue, they can be gradually encouraged to change things a little. This is the direct opposite of so much that happens in current French teaching. In the example conversations, movement towards a basic naturalness can be achieved by omitting (or leaving the option to omit) much of the artificial repetition we are prone to use in an attempt to inculcate structure. It is not surprising that the children are often bemused by the need to repeat the structure used in the question in French, when they would almost never do so in English. How does the reader feel about the following piece of conversation for someone learning English as a foreign language?

What is your name? ... My name is Francisco Gomez ... How old are you? ... I am twelve years old ... Are you Spanish? ... Yes, I am Spanish ... Do you live in England? ... Yes, I live in England

... Do you live in a house? ... No, I do not live in a house. I live in a flat ... Do you come to school by car? ... Yes, I come to school by car.

One doubts there is any need for comment.

And yet there is no disputing the fact that structure must be practised in conversation. How can the more natural flow of language in the examples **a**, **b** and **c** help, when it and the strong words above seem to exclude the practising of structure? It does help and does not exclude practice. What it tries to exclude is unnecessary, artificial repetition of structure on a too frequent basis.

What, then, is being substituted? Only material that is less confusing and the opportunity for the whole class (or at least a group) to practise at the same time, instead of having to listen for ten to fifteen minutes while other pairs practise individually at the front of the class. In the situation that we are all familiar with, perhaps a third of the class will have one chance to say something in a quarter of an hour.

Extra practice is given in the method advocated by the reversal of roles. This ordinary enough device gives **B** a chance to work through the structures **A** has been using and vice versa. Additionally, the class takes less time to achieve a reasonable standard of production of the dialogue and more conversations can be assimilated in the space of a term than by the standard method. It is in this extra time available that the teacher can find the opportunity to practise structure even further by introducing it into other dialogues. Short and sweet, meaningful dialogues score every time. For all the advantage gleaned by the change of method the conversations are still, of necessity, stylised, but the simplicity and natural rhythm of the paired dialogues can be so advantageous because they allow the pupils a basic flexibility in their use of their second language.

Again, this sounds very fine, since one does not usually look for any sort of flexibility at an early stage of language learning. With simple conversational material however, the individual can be encouraged to dare a little. When the teacher feels a dialogue is tolerably well known by the class, he might now actively encourage them to change things. In conversation **b**, for example, it is quite easy to introduce an element of pretence. Many children will need little persuasion to pretend they are someone else—a celebrity, sportsman, Uncle Joe, Auntie Florrie—or to change their age to something outlandish, and to invent brothers and sisters. And once they start this, they are beginning to forget about the language, if only for a couple of minutes a week. The second language is beginning to become behaviour and to approach the way people function in their mother tongue.

Trying conversations on the level of pretending is particularly open to the criticism of actively encouraging language error. It is only too true that a deal of ungrammatical and mispronounced French will be produced during free and, arguably, controlled group work. One can easily imagine the errors present with a group practising five short conversations in the space of five to seven minutes, even though they are supposed to be very familiar with the material.

It is impossible for the teacher to monitor more than a fraction of what is being spoken as he does his round of the groups, but this is not a wholly valid reason for refusing to allow group paired-conversations. Any fixing in the child's mind of incorrect language patterns is offset by the increase in vocabulary, fluency and other structure that all the extra opportunity to speak allows. Sufficient correction can be done through the increased opportunity the teacher has to hear each child speaking over a period of a year, and the groups can be encouraged into a surprisingly high degree of self-correction, if we will only allow them to get into the habit.

Also, it should not be forgotten that the vast amount of extra spoken practice that such strategies allow can, in fact, permit the teacher to spend less time on oral work than is very often the case with early learners if he so wishes, and use the time saved for basic reading or copy-writing practice. Indeed, if after the first few months of French the average class is being submitted to a totally oral lesson, then as far as concentration and effort are concerned we are asking too much of the child. Paired conversations allow a large amount of concentrated practice and leave time for other things. After all, we have recently been reminded that the overall level of pupil achievement in French might not be that high. One should not be afraid to try something new, as long as it is carefully prepared and instituted.

The final question to consider is the degree of noise engendered. This will always be something of a problem. In a subject where, in the initial stages at least, the teacher is concentrating on encouraging the pupil to learn to speak, it is patently unrealistic to expect a class to be as quiet as when they are, for example, writing up a science field visit. If one is going to encourage oral confidence, the children can hardly be expected to polish their metaphorical teeth in near silence. Yet, if we are experienced teachers and have never taught any French we already know that, up to early adolescence, excessive noise springs mostly from the pupils' not knowing what they have to do, not having enough to occupy them, and not being interested in what they are doing. Ways of countering these factors are examined at various stages in this manual, so at this point it is worth studying another factor that is really quite peculiar to modern language teaching, or at least to the particular approach to oral work at present under consideration. Not only is the teacher encouraging children to speak for a far longer part of the lesson time than would normally be the case in other subject areas, but group paired conversations actively channel the whole of the class into speaking at the same time.

Thus, if everybody is talking at anything more than whisper level, the noise has to increase.

In the past, people accepted the necessity for table-chanting in mathematics lessons and even in the French teaching field many teachers would seem to employ choral repetition after and without the tape recorder. The heart of this particular problem is not the fact of thirty people talking at the same time, so much as what happens when they have the chance to express themselves verbally in exclusive duets and isolate themselves from the rest of the class.

In this connection, it is optimistic to believe that good discipline and insistence on quiet speech will produce the desired results. They may well, particularly if the individual teacher is consistently determined in his approach. Equally, they may well not. Still, there are practical steps one can take to allow the average teacher a much fairer chance of success.

Most colleagues will be all too aware of how noise fluctuates with the actual classroom and time-table conditions. Why not, then, try to ensure that potentially noisy activities coincide with those periods when the children are at their most quiescent? With an average class, immediately after a games lesson is not the best time to situate free oral work. Neither is the latter end of Friday, when the children are even more aware of the impending weekend than we are. But after a quiet reading activity may be just the right time.

Given consistency, a sensitive attitude to timing, and a regular pattern of work that does not confuse the class, progress should be made with free oral sessions.

If, on the other hand, one still cannot countenance the thought of even trying out the class on such a technique as paired conversations, the group work pattern can be organised so as to have only one group working in pairs at any one time. If during this activity one concentrates one's monitoring upon a particular group, a maximum of eight people talking at the same time will not make things impossible for the rest of the class. Such a strategy also has the advantage of easing the teacher's apprehension with regard to the increased grammatical inaccuracies discussed earlier.

It is one thing to try dividing the class into groups working on what is basically the same material, with some concessions made to the varying ability levels. It is something of a very different order to have, say, five groups in the one room working independently on a variety of activities reflecting the heterogeneous nature of our single class—even if it is streamed. It is now time to look at the specific relevance of this teaching strategy to the capacities—intellectual, academic and social—of the children in our charge. The following chapters offer practical suggestions for developing such capacities within the French lesson.

Chapter 2

Mixed Ability Teaching

A class teacher in a small primary school suddenly finds him or herself a semi-specialist in French at the same school, or the new middle school; the secondary modern and grammar school teachers become comprehensive school teachers almost overnight. They have to cope with different pupils or aims, very often with one standard set of unsuitable course materials and little money available to buy afresh. With such a scenario it is doubtful whether many colleagues can guarantee to be teaching the same type of children with the same aims in mind in just five years' time.

If only a methodology could be developed that would allow sufficient flexibility to enable the teacher to change with the times, not in any modish way, but merely to adapt to the changing demands of changing institutions. None can claim to have perfected such a method, but independent group work within class can help to save the French teacher's sanity and the interest, participation and potential of the children.

Mixed, random and streamed abilities are three very divergent approaches to school structuring, with the basic raw material of the developing human being as their common resource. Can independent group work, containing very large elements of individualised learning, allow children to learn at their own pace? If so, the argument over streaming and non-streaming would be largely defused.

What exactly is independent group work? The approach to working in groups that we have examined thus far relies on the unit material introduced and taught by the teacher as the basis of whatever activities are devised. Independent group work is a compromise with such fixed-centre assignments, with the aim of allowing the various groupings within the class to follow different materials and units of work, according to their ability, knowledge, interests and levels of performance.

A fundamental truth of the method lies in the fact that if the child is given the opportunity to work broadly at his or her own pace, this in itself constitutes a form of setting, since the pupil finds his own level and largely sets himself.

There are, of course, very practical reasons why one should be encouraged into adopting this flexible type of approach, and such practicalities tend to centre on what we might call the 'one-level' approach of most commercial courses. Commercial materials need to be made flexible and this is even true of a course designed for a high ability class. Performance in French is not uniform in a first year top stream and one often hears how grammar school 'C' stream pupils are said to be 'not up to' taking French. Course books do not always help the teacher preparing pupils for public examinations. There is then a need for flexible French at all levels.

A major difficulty is the responsibility for assessment that the method throws on the teacher. No-one likes having the feeling of playing God with the children and their futures, when making the decision that Jim is of such and such an ability and will therefore work on this programme in that group. But flexible French should not just allow us flexibility of materials. One of the very real advantages of independent group activities is the opportunity they offer to re-assess the child's level, according to the progress he or she makes. If, for example, Jennifer is making surprising headway on bottom-ability work (whether she is working singly with a random-grouping, or along with the other members of a bottom-ability group), she can be tried on the work that is being done by the next ability level up (see Chapter 4, page 44).

Linked to the fear of taking wrong decisions about children's abilities is the apprehension that, feeling one's way towards a freer system, one may free machinery to such an extent that it will be impossible to put it back together again. The teacher suspects a lack of direction will ensue and that he will be following wrong progress targets and study areas. This is a most understandable reaction. How can he ensure meeting these objections at least partially?

He needs to have a starting point from which to develop each week or fortnight's work. The best way to achieve this with the minimum of fuss and searching is to take the basic unit of the commercial course. If, for example, he has a genuine mixed ability class containing some very able and some poor ability children plus a middle grouping of average children, and the course materials are aimed at the average child, then he needs to think of activities for the two extremes in class. He concentrates his additionally prepared activities on the top and bottom and these are loosely or closely linked to the central theme.

Similarly, one might find oneself if the not too infrequent situation, where a one-time small grammar school has become the junior end of a 11–18 comprehensive or high school and the course materials left for use are more suitable for the more able children in the school. The teacher would normally be dealing with thirteen year olds, who would have had between eighteen months and three years experience of French. Almost certainly there is unlikely to be any uniformity in the amount of French teaching the children will have had, unless the school has been able to institute some setting scheme, to balance the pupils according to their experience and ability. With such a variety in the amount of French experience within the class, courses and textbooks are expected to do a job which they are fundamentally incapable of achieving, despite their individual excellence.

Les Routes de campagne!

M. Durandet a acheté une nouvelle voiture pour sa famille et tous les Durandet en sont bien contents. Et, qu'est-ce qu'ils ont comme nouvelle voiture? Regardez l'image et vous allez reconnaître le dernier modèle de Renault, qui monte facilement à 180 kilomètres à l'heure.

Les Durandet n'ont pas toujours aimé faire des excursions à la campagne, mais maintenant, ils adorent les pique-niques. Un beau samedi matin, ils ont pris leur petit déjeuner à sept heures et demie, et puis ils ont fait les préparatifs pour leur promenade en voiture...

Mais, les routes de campagne, vous savez, ce ne sont pas toujours faciles! Pauvre M. Durandet, sa belle Renault a sauté drôlement sur cette route départementale, et enfin a cessé de marcher juste devant un petit pont! Lui et Michel ont vérifié les pneus. Pas de problèmes. Ils ont examiné toute la voiture et n'ont rien trouvé. «Je ne comprends pas!» a dit M. Durandet. «C'est peut-être l'essence?» a demandé sa femme. «Impossible!» a répondu son mari et il a regardé l'indicateur du réservoir. Vous pouvez deviner le reste – les femmes ont toujours raison!

Fig. 3 Les Routes de campagne

Fig. 3 is a reasonably faithful reflection of the type of passage found in commercial courses for early practice in the *Passé Composé*. It illustrates how well-conceived single-level courses cannot possibly cope with all the levels of pupil experience and ability thrown at them. The reason is that linking the Perfect verbs is a variety of linguistic items many of which will be too complex or sophisticated for the average-to-weak pupil, despite the apparent simplicity of the story-line. In the circumstances outlined above, the course materials cannot be judged fairly. It is therefore imperative to try to use the course in the most effective way that the situation permits. One accepts that the original passage and its standard written exercises will form the basis of a perfectly satisfactory work programme for the more able, but will still have to do some individual work on it with this group, because, as so often happens, the course books have been purchased, but not the filmstrips or tapes. The middle band in the class will find considerable difficulty in coping with the exercises on the Perfect Tense that follow the narrative and one will recently have introduced them to the concept of the new tense, without dwelling lengthily on it and without aiming at written attempts at reproduction at this stage.

If, however, the essential vocabulary is extracted and use made of the fact that the passage divides neatly into sections, there is much that can be done.

Although the tapes are not available the teacher may be able to obtain the services of a local French person, or the Assistant(e), who could tape the text and an adapted version of the comprehension questions that occur in the Teacher's Book, e.g.

Les Routes de campagne! – Questions

1 Pourquoi les Durandet sont-ils contents?
2 Décrivez un peu la voiture.
3 Est-çe que les Durandet ont toujours adoré les pique-niques?
4 A quelle heure est-ce qu'ils ont mangé?
5 Et qu'est-ce qu'ils ont fait après?
6 Comment la belle Renault est-ce qu'elle a roulé sur les routes de campagne?
7 Où est-ce que la voiture a cessé de marcher?
8 Qu'est-ce que M. Durandet et Michel ont examiné d'abord?
9 Et qu'est-ce qu'ils ont trouvé?
10 Qu'est-ce que M. Durandet a fait pour vérifier l'essence?
11 Pourquoi est-ce que la voiture a cessé de marcher?

Fig. 4

With some taped material, the scope of the lesson is immediately increased. But before proceeding to use the tape, the teacher remembers the basic requirement to test one skill at a time at the start. This is vital. What is meant by single-skill testing? If the pupils were required to familiarise themselves with the text, listen to the questions and then answer them orally or in written form in French, then one would be attempting to test more than one skill in the foreign language—to understand the written and spoken word and to speak or write. There is no reason why one should not build up to double-skill work, but with pupils other than the higher ability groups, it makes sound sense to work on one skill at a time. For instance, to listen to sections of the tape of the text and answers questions in French immediately afterwards would be demanding for those of average ability and experience. If however they were to hear the tape in French with the questions in English and were allowed to answer in English, this would provide a basis for further work up to questions and replies in French.

Using a French or English question-answer pattern, the teacher can provide further activity by dividing the group into pairs, getting **A** to repeat the French question posed on tape and **B** to answer in English (later in French). When the group starts on the catechism, the teacher will be there directing and then monitoring. After he has moved on to another group, the previous group should be able to carry on working independently with the tape recorder, provided it is a cassette and battery-powered, for reasons of safety.

The question of teacher-movement during group work is crucial to the strategy. He will not merely circulate checking on what the groups have been producing spontaneously under their own steam. There will, of course, be parts of the pupils' French work where they will apply themselves in a very free and independent manner, but given the nature of second-language learning and the problems of acquisition, children cannot be allowed to proceed totally on a 'learning by discovery' basis, working solely on sub-topics that interest them within a very loosely built framework. As we have seen with the question-and-answer routine outlined above, each group has to receive a certain amount of specific teaching within the week, whether it is progressive or remedial. The requirement for some teacher-based instruction subsists, since the children's progress depends partly on our experience of French.

Perhaps the group lesson-cycle instanced below will be of help in illustrating how it is perfectly feasible to maintain an ordered sequence of activities in which both pupils and teacher will know their place, and which ensures that the teacher distributes his monitoring and servicing time realistically.

The five groups rotate clockwise through a five-period cycle and move physically from one area to the next after each lesson, or when it is decided the change is required. Although this means some disturbance, it is better than the dislocation caused by moving the equipment with the children. The system is sufficiently flexible to allow a variety of modifications, e.g. group work-units can be only fifteen minutes long if so desired, group activities can be halted in the middle of a lesson for a whole-class teaching-point, and the teacher may allow himself generous monitoring time for the rest of the class if he so wishes, by ensuring that his work-area commitment only takes up half of the group work time available.

Independent group work, then, does not imply that the various groups are progressing all the time independently of the teacher, but rather that the groups are independent of each other, working on their own material. The fact that the teacher will have some teaching to do with all the groups, albeit separately, will have implications for the class disposition. If the pupils are grouped by ability there will be no problem in the sense that, to carry out the planned teaching with a particular set of children, the teacher will only have to be on the spot to find all those with whom he

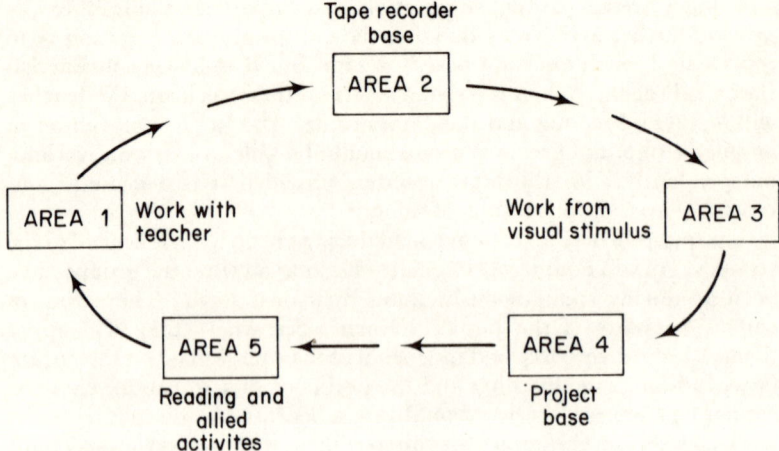

Fig. 5 A Group Cycle. Arrows indicate group rotation. Except for the Project base, a new group arriving at a work area will find different activities from the last, according to their abilities and level of learning, e.g. the most able group could expect to spend some of its time at each area on written work in French.

should be currently concerned in the one area of the classroom. If however it is a class of random groupings, uniform groupings will have to be produced for the teaching time and also, possibly, for any follow-up activities. If, for example, the pupils are to practise pair discussions after the teaching session, they are best kept together rather than re-dispersed in pairs, only to disturb by their conversation others who are working quietly.

To return to the not-so-hypothetical class. After the initial question-and-answer routine, the middle-ability children are beginning to develop a reasonable general understanding of the passage, thanks also to some *Remplissez les Blancs!* work cards, which they complete without the benefit of the text in front of them immediately after hearing relevant sections of the passage read through (see pp. 33, 34 and 36). As an alternative to the narrative coming from the tape recorder, the teacher may be tempted to use someone from the top ability band to read out the material.

The teacher now feels the time has come for the middle band to move on from their text, or rather to use it as a basis for some copy-writing of, and continued familiarisation with, the written form of the new tense. Over the years, the class-teacher has built up a stock of picture cuttings of all shapes, sizes and descriptions from Paris Match, the Sunday supplements, and mail order catalogues. As a result of such conscientious stockpiling, it is a relatively simple matter to find a dozen pictures portraying actions that are present in the written text. The middle band of pupils consists of two groups of six, so each group has half the pictures and they exchange when they have finished with their particular pictures. The activity is a straightforward exercise called *Qu'est-ce qu'il a fait?/Qu'est-ce qu'elle a fait?*, in which the children have to extract from the passage the sentence to match the picture and write it down. At this stage, many may consider it advisable that the sentence be exactly transferable, as what is being aimed at is copy-writing with a small element of challenge.

As a final element if the children are making good progress, the pictures with the most straightforward accompanying titles may be represented the following lesson, this time without any text, and the children challenged to recall and write down the exact sentence.

With the lower-ability third of the class, the position is essentially very different. Such material as *Les Routes de Campagne* is already beyond them and it is some months since the decision has been made to abandon any attempt to keep up with the rest of the class. The pace has been diminished, but not yet the distant objective of a reasonable total of meaningful progress in French. Gradually, the teacher is increasing what might be termed the 'survival element' in this band's curriculum, though the major part of their work is still remedial language. Every week teaching-time is devoted to re-covering ground from the previous year.

The most intractable problem with these children, many of whom, by common consent, are often amongst the nicest people in the class, is their inability to concentrate for anything longer than very short periods. To this is linked their need for greater attention. All of which means that if the teacher is not careful he will be splitting himself in many different directions, trying to do his best for everyone all of the time.

The less able pupil's problem when it comes to concentrating is one reason why he or she has to be given diversionary tasks. With some thought, these can often be linked to the topic areas the class are concerned with. They can, for example, take the form of information-finding, keeping a scrapbook, or something specifically relevant to the development of the week's work.

After *Les Routes de Campagne!* the majority of the class would be moving on to work with *Le Code de la Route*. This is a study area which is made very much easier with a working model and so for the last fortnight, the bottom band will have been spending some of their time assembling a model town-layout and making appropriate street and road signs. Ideally however, a balance has to be struck with such activities, not only in the sense that one must try to achieve the right ratio of tasks for lower ability children, but also for the simple fact that they must not be allowed to monopolise all the modelmaking or other obviously pleasurable activities.

The need for greater attention is partially satisfied by the feeling of importance the less able pupils obtain by making and doing things for the class. However, there is another form of attention that they will need and that is the constant encouraging or chivvying along and the reassurance that they are doing the right thing. The teacher just cannot be with them all the time.

One frequent positive result of the group-based class is an increase in mutual tolerance and a corresponding decrease in overt rivalry. Given these twain, top ability and middle ability pupils can become very prepared to help out with the bottom groups and if this is done on an organised basis, both ends of the class benefit considerably from such cooperation. The quarter of an hour 'given up' once a month by a pupil to help with the less-able (or late-comers), is more than offset by the revision practice it affords. As far as feelings of embarrassment and insignificance are concerned, these can be countered by the fact that there are very often some people in the lower groups who are only there by reason of their late start with French or prolonged absence due to illness, and by the sheer logicality of giving them (and, therefore, their group-mates) extra practice and attention in order for them to make the progress of which they are capable.

Again, the question of the late arrival, of the new child with no French and of the pupil returning after lengthy illness, illustrates the flexibility of the group work system. Without it, most children in these three categories would find it difficult to reach even the average level of performance within the class, unless they were highly able or equally determined. But with distinct groups operating and even the possibility of creating special groups, if there are enough children to warrant it, such pupils have the chance of making up lost ground, according to their capacities.

Chapter 3

Group Activities

Oral Techniques

Oral techniques are the first area to be dealt with, since it is spoken activities in group work that tend to arouse the greatest scepticism and are undoubtedly the most difficult to organise, administer and maintain. Disorganised oral/aural work is a recipe for chaos. The obligation therefore exists to find activities that are sufficiently interesting, demanding, time-consuming and appropriate, for the inevitable rise in volume that accompanies mass oral work to be kept within acceptable levels.

Similarly, to offset the other possible negative effects of group oral work—increased opportunity for bad, uncorrected spoken French; lack of supervision—the teacher makes sure that the new group activities contain sufficient variety in vocabulary, information and general utility and challenge, for the five or seven minutes devoted to them to be sufficient to help, test, motivate and stretch the pupils.

At the same time as one lists the obvious pitfalls inherent in group oral work, one should remember the equally inherent advantages, which are rarely present in teacher-based oral lessons.

The fact that the teacher is always in control of the language being produced is a limiting factor, because *a* he and/or the children demonstrating in front of the class are always striving to produce exactly the language he wants, and *b* children generally speak much more effectively in peer-groupings and peer-situations. Given the group situation, the child has more opportunity of achieving what he or she is capable of in their second language. The teacher is clearly an inhibiting factor and once the basic material has been practised, the less teacher impinges the better. Additionally, on the more intimate group level, it is much easier for the teacher to function as a correctant and encourager in a more subdued and relaxed manner than in whole-class situations.

The other major advantage implicit in group oral strategies and alluded to elsewhere, is the opportunity afforded to the child of balanced conversation. No matter how able the teacher performing in a teacher-based situation, there is always the tendency for teacher to ask and pupil to answer. Even when such a lesson is varied by a demonstration group at the front, it is often normal for one child to be fed the questions while the others answer.

Yet if we perform the simple experiment in English of dividing the class into pairs and asking them to initiate a conversation on any topic they like, we will discover that somewhere near half the dialogue is in the interrogative.

It is essential that the child be able to ask questions in French. Being just able to answer them is not good enough. Not only is it not good enough, it is also highly counterproductive, since it does not take the average child long to realise how artificial the second language situation is when he or she is being fed questions to answer as if they are appearing in a television contest.

In such a situation, group oral activities properly administered can bring a change almost overnight for the very reason that, because the teacher is left out of the equation, balanced conversations between the children are the immediate target. With such equal catechisms in mind, the example activities below should prove helpful.

1 Basic Question and Answer Routine (Teacher-Controlled)

A start is made with a teacher-controlled activity, to facilitate a phased introduction consistent with the principle of gradual acclimatisation.

The teacher stands at the front of the class, with a set of flashcards illustrating the current language teaching point. The leader of each group, henceforth referred to as the *animateur*, has a similar set of cards with matching questions and answers written on the back. During the first run-through the teacher, holding up the relevant card, may ask the question, for it to be repeated to the group by the animateur. As the answer is in front of him or her, the *animateur* or *animatrice* can correct a group-member if the right answer has not been given. The teacher holds up the whole series of cards, one by one, and questions are asked round the group. The next lesson, there is a change of *animateur* on the basis of a number rota, which avoids confusion and debate. If the teacher feels sufficiently confident that the class can cope, he may feel that the questions can be asked by the *animateur* without putting them first himself. On the other hand, there is a strong argument for this type of half-way activity with some teacher reinforcement in the early stages. Indeed, many may feel they would wish to continue with a fairly high degree of teacher involvement in such oral activities, even when the children are experienced, confident and competent, on the basis that a little intervention by themselves, before the children move to the next stage of practising the material completely on their own, is likely to have a beneficial effect on the children's solo performance.

Central to the ethos of this form of assignment is the fact that what is

2 C'est toi, le coupable! (Descriptive Discovery)

This activity encourages accurate questioning and description and is flexible enough to be used even to adult level. Assuming a group of six, each member is given a small booklet (a vocabulary book cut in half, or in quarters) and, during a free lesson or wet playtime, the groups letter their booklets **A–F**, number the pages 1–6 on the back, and draw the objects on the front of the numbered pages, representing the contents of their *cartables*, as specified in the table below (Fig. 6).

We now have the elements for a detection game, with a policeman/detective, one thief and four innocent individuals. The game is played with each member of the group at the same page in his or her *carnet*. You will see from the Table that there are a different *détective* and *voleur* for each page. It is also evident that, because there is always some similarity between the page that the detective has before him with the stolen object(s) on it and the other five pages, he has to be very careful in his interrogation of his five subjects if he is to find out who is guilty, especially if the rules are arranged so that the detective loses if the wrong person is accused.

The game can be varied in that the duty detective may concentrate his or her interrogation on one person at a time and eliminate them from the enquiry, or random questioning around the group may be allowed. Whatever the rules, the scope is large.

An example interrogation, centring on Page 1 of the carnet:

Pupil **B**: *Je cherche un billet de dix francs et une montre, Marc (= **A**). Tu as un billet dans ton cartable?*
Pupil **A**: *Oui, j'ai un billet.*
    B: *De combien?*
    A: *De dix francs.*
    B: *Est-ce que tu as une montre?*
    A: *Non, je n'ai pas de montre.*
    B: *Tu as autre chose?*
    A: *Non, rien.*
    B: *Alors, ce n'est pas toi!*
    B: *Je cherche un billet de dix francs et une montre. Jean (= **C**), combien de choses as-tu dans ton cartable?*
    C: *J'en ai deux.*
    B: *Tu as de l'argent?*
    C: *Peut-être!*
    B: *Oui ou non?*
    C: *Oui.*

PUPIL	PAGE 1	PAGE 2	PAGE 3	PAGE 4	PAGE 5	PAGE 6
A	Un billet de dix francs	° Une boîte de cigares	Deux sifflets et un bâton d'agent	* Un collier de perles et un bracelet d'or	Une bouteille rouge et une boîte jaune	Une blouse bleue et une paire de bottes jaunes
B	* Un billet de dix francs et une montre	Deux boîtes de cigares	Un sifflet	Un collier de perles	° Une bouteille jaune et une boîte rouge	Un tricot bleu et une paire de souliers jaunes
C	Un billet de cinquante francs et une montre	Une boîte de cigarettes	* Un sifflet et un bâton d'agent	° Un collier de perles et un bracelet d'or	Une boîte rouge	Une chemise bleue et une paire de chaussettes jaunes
D	° Un billet de dix francs et une montre	Une boîte de cigares et un briquet	Un sifflet, un bâton d'agent et un képi	Un collier d'or et un bracelet de perles	Une bouteille bleue et une boîte orange	* Un tricot bleu et une paire de chaussettes jaunes
E	Un billet de dix francs et deux montres	* Une boîte de cigares	Un bâton d'agent	Un bracelet d'or	Une bouteille jaune	° Un tricot bleu et une paire de chaussettes jaunes
F	Une montre	Une boîte de tabac	° Un sifflet et un bâton d'agent	Un collier de chien et un bracelet pour montre	* Une bouteille jaune et une boîte rouge	Un tricot bleu et une paire de bottes jaunes

Fig. 6 C'est toi le coupable!

* Le détective
° Le coupable

B: *Tu as une montre?*
C: *Oui, j'ai une montre.*
B: *Alors, c'est toi, le voleur!*
C: *Non, ce n'est pas moi. J'ai un billet de cinquante francs!*
B: *Zut, j'ai perdu!*

The conversation above, or something approximate to it, is within the reach of a pupil towards the end of his or her first year of French, but one would not expect such dialogues to proceed without mistakes. Gradually, though, with the teacher monitoring the groups, they will have sufficient practice to eliminate many of the inevitable mistakes and to produce a considerable amount of spoken French.

One of the difficulties with this type of assignment is the way in which it does allow answering pupils to produce one-word responses, but if the teacher works on the principle of encouraging the groups not to be deliberately obstructive by replying in monosyllables, this tendency can be countered. Also, as the role of detective moves round the group, each member will have had considerable oral practice over two or three group sessions.

A problem with all group oral activities is that of preventing the excessive use of English by the pupils. Speaking no English once the activity has started, can be made a point of honour, with the reinforcement that if the exercise is a points-scoring activity, the English-talkers lose their score. Judgement is to be given by the members of the group.

The composite table given as an example of such an interrogation activity contains a mixture of vocabulary levels and little tricks. With a first year group, after only a few months of French, one might consider it sensible not to have too many distractors in the pictures and to concentrate, for example, on colour, with two straightforward items of clothing, *une cravate* and *une blouse*. As page 6 of the illustration stands, scope for misinterpretation on several levels has been introduced.

3 Sur le Plan! (Map Description)

Another flexible oral activity demanding precise description and questioning, *Sur le Plan!* can be adapted to the level required, be it First or Sixth Form. The example dialogue is from a class of twelve to thirteen year olds.

The group *animateur* has a master *plan*, which is divided into four numbered quarters (see Fig. 7, below).

All the other members of the group have a blank, quartered map. The *animateur* begins describing what is on his master copy (hidden from the group) and the others start drawing in their map. He deals with the objects on the map, one at a time, and his colleagues are allowed to ask questions so they can locate each object precisely. The aim is to produce

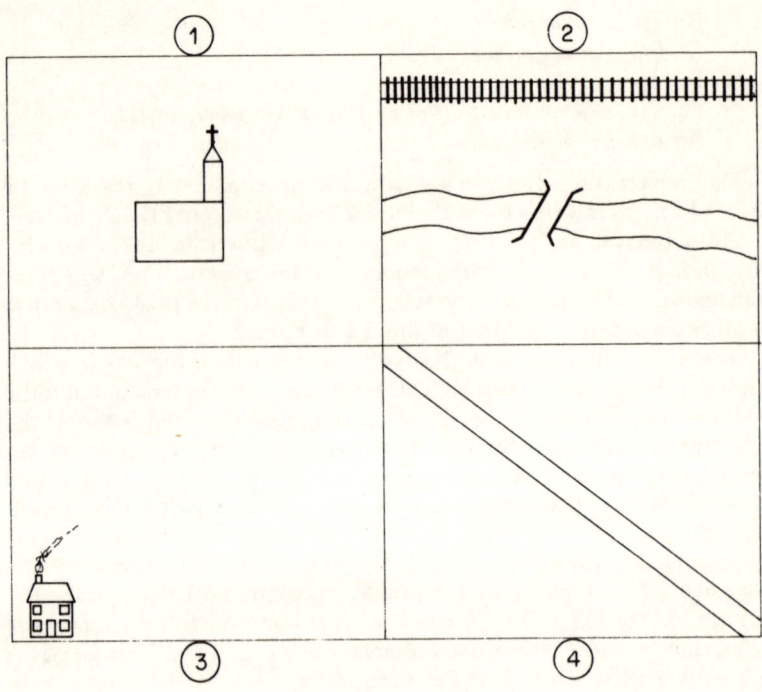

Fig. 7 Master plan

a nearly exact copy of the original. The ensuing conversation in a class familiar with the activity would run approximately thus:

 Dans le premier carré, il y a une église.
  —Où? En haut, à droite?
Non, au milieu.
 Dans le troisième, il y a une maison.
  —A gauche?
Oui, mais en bas.
  —Tout en bas?
Oui, sur la ligne.
 Dans le deuxième, il y a un chemin de fer en haut, qui va de gauche à droite.
  —C'est tout?
Non, il y a aussi une rivière au milieu, avec un pont au milieu.
 Dans numéro quatre, il y a une route qui descend.
  —Au milieu?
Non, elle descend en diagonale.
  —De droite à gauche?
Non, de gauche à droite.

If there is not enough time for this to be a drawing activity, the group can make their own little symbols and place them on the blank map. The basic activity can clearly be adapted for a variety of assignments, on a grid system—the description of a room, the location of various individuals in hiding, to name only the most obvious.

A major advantage of Activities 2 and 3 over much conventional conversation work is the way in which they are based on something solid and the pupils are not talking into the air. Allied to this is the principle that, for the children to reach the goal of the activity, there is a positive need to speak, a specific requirement to seek out information. There is also scope for interplay of personality, should the teacher wish to encourage it, in that the children may be allowed to make the games more difficult for each other by hiding information, uttering misleading statements and leading on by facial gesture. This latter element is a welcome addition to the usually low level of non-verbal communication built in to the children's second language experience.

4 Faites bien Attention!

This exercise is a form of sentence repetition, containing an element of challenge. The *animateur* has a card with a series of sentences, based on the work of the last week or so, with one word omitted from each. The activity is a contest between the *animateur* and the rest of the group, with the latter allowed only three guesses to complete each sentence after it has been read out.

Faites bien Attention!   **Animateur/trice**

Read out each sentence twice, WITHOUT filling in the gaps from the brackets. Go round the group one by one, starting on your left and allowing THREE attempts only to say the complete sentence. The team score one point for each correct sentence and you score the same for each one they do not get right.

1 Il y a des _____ noirs. (nuages)
2 Il fait du _____. (vent)
3 Il va _____. (pleuvoir)
4 La _____ commence dans dix minutes. (pièce)
5 Nous allons _____ en retard. (arriver)
6 J'ai _____ les Duclos ce matin. (rencontré)
7 Ils vont _____ une voiture de sport. (acheter)
8 Attention, tu vas _____! (tomber)
9 _____ vais en Angleterre. (je)
10 Hélène va en _____. (Allemagne)

Fig. 8

5 On recherche ...!

Each member of the group has his or her own numbered card placed in front of them on the table or desk, so the individuals are known by their numbers to the rest of the group. In the middle is a pile of cards, face down. Each member takes a card in turn, without looking underneath first and making sure no-one else can see what is written on it. They then take their turn at describing their allotted individuals, without looking at them.

The person they describe is a wanted criminal. If the describer can make four statements about their subject before he or she is guessed, or induce someone into making a wrong guess, they score a point, otherwise the point goes to the one who guesses correctly. Questions must be put, and guesses made, in order round the group.

On recherche ...!

The usual rules: If you are unsure what these are, check in your « Activités! » notebook. But REMEMBER, don't make the description too obvious.

SUBJECT: PETER ("POP") ROBSON

BASIC DETAILS
Onze ans ... cheveux blonds ... habite Belsay ... l'équipe de rugby ... deux frères ... mange beaucoup ... partisan de Newcastle United ... la pêche ... deuxième prénom Alf.

What other details can you tell them in French?

Fig. 9 On recherche ...!

6 Non!

Non! is a similar strategy in reverse. Each person picks a card with the name of another group member on it. The group ask questions of you, to find out who the person on your card is. If you can answer *Non!* to a question, then the group has lost. This discourages wild guessing and encourages longer and more thoughtful questions.

> e.g. *Est-ce que cette personne va à l'école à pied, à vélo, ou en autobus?* is relatively safe, whereas *Il va à l'école à pied?* has a much greater chance of the answer *Non!*

7 Les Huiles! (The V.I.P.s!)

There is a pile of picture cards of class members and famous people in the middle of the table. The *animateur* selects a card, looks at the picture, and keeps it hidden from the rest of the group, who have to ask questions to identify the mystery person. *Les Huiles!* is a useful strategy to introduce after the children are familiar with *On recherche...!* and *Non!*, since it offers an immediately wider vocabulary and general *civilisation* range, together with considerable opportunity for structure practice, e.g.:

> *C'est un homme ou une femme?*
> —*Ni l'un, ni l'autre.*
> *Un garçon ou une fille, alors?*
> —*Non plus.*
> *Ça doit être un animal?*
> —*Naturellement.*
> *On le voit à la télé?*
> —*Ça dépend.*
> *Alors, on l'entend à la radio?*
> —*C'est possible.*
> *Cet animal, de quelle couleur est-il?*
> —*Blanc.*
> *C'est Crin Blanc!*
> —*Ça y est!*

The comment likely to be made on such a catechism is that it is too advanced for the average thirteen to fourteen year old (and beyond). But, on closer inspection, one sees that it is perfectly attainable and that most of what is said is what one might term the conventional language of such an interrogation. What is doubly useful with many games and activities is that they contain their own linguistic conventions, which can be initially taught and gradually acquired. The acquisition occurs because the pupil needs conventions like *Ça doit être...* , or *On l'entend à la radio?* to perform effectively in an activity which is challenging and in which, with a little luck, he will become absorbed. For the linguistician, this is the type of exercise where the pupil is positively encouraged to produce *parole* rather than *langue*, i.e. the language itself is being adapted to fit with the pupil's intended behaviour. He or she is selecting what should be said, to achieve a particular rather subtle end, as in the use of *Ni l'un, ni l'autre, Non plus, Naturellement, Ça dépend* and *C'est possible* to deliberately deflect, distract, confuse and dominate. The situation has provided scope for language in action.

8 Cloze Activities

Cloze activities are another very flexible device. Cloze sentences are those where an item is omitted at regular intervals, e.g. one word in three, or in six. The wider the interval between omissions, the easier it will be to fill the gaps in the sentence. Thus, by varying the omission gaps, one can produce linguistic games that are challenging for bottom and top ability groups at all ages. Equally useful is the fact that sentences can be so structured as to allow the gaps to be used to practise specific teaching-points.

For the example group activity, the *animateur* has a set of cards, or a single card, with a series of sentences containing a gap every fourth word. He works round the group, letting each member complete one gap at a time, with one point scored for every correct guess. It is important, of course, to make sure that the missing words are written in at the bottom or side of the card(s), so that the *animateur* has all the answers.

Un sur quatre!

Animateur – *read out the sentences below, leaving gaps where they are shown. Starting with the person on your left, let each person answer one gap. One point for each correct answer. If wrong or no answer given, pass to next person. (Answers given in brackets after each sentence)*

1 A sept heures _____ réveil sonne dans _____ chambre. (le, la)
2 Je me réveille _____ sept heures vingt _____ je vais à _____ ferme. (à, quand/si, la)
3 Papa va au _____ dans sa grande _____. (bureau, voiture)
4 Mets le timbre _____ l'enveloppe.   (sur)
5 Quand il fait _____ je nage dans _____ piscine. (chaud, la)
6 Comment vous appelez _____? Je m'appelle _____. (vous, *answerer's name*)
7 Donnez-moi un _____ de sucre et _____ demi-kilo de _____ secs. (kilo, un, gâteaux)
8 Boris est un _____ qui adore aller _____ cinéma. (garçon, au)

Fig. 10

Cloze work is often found to be a particularly good activity for overcoming the pupils' antipathy to re-practice. A group can be got to go through the above card four or five times without its losing all its freshness, if the *animateur* ensures that a different person starts each time, so that pupils are constantly having to fill in different gaps from the last time around. This is good practice. One notices how it induces the learner into paying attention to individual words and their role in the sentence.

9 A la Fin!
With this completion exercise, only one word, the last, is consistently missing from the sentence. Again, it promotes careful listening.

    e.g. *A 4h.30, le train part de la ...*
        M. Duval va à l'aéroport pour prendre un ...
        Un vélo a deux ...
        Le fermier travaille dans les champs avec son ...

Un solex est un vélo avec un petit ...
La R4 est une petite ...
Ily y a deux sortes de bus—un autobus, et un ...
Pour transporter un malade à l'hôpital, appelez une ...
(Based on a transport project, done with an early second year class.)

The *animateur* has a card with the unfinished sentences and their completions written on, and the activity is once again practised several times, with a different starter on each occasion. In addition, such oral activities are a useful base for copy-writing. When the sentences have been thoroughly practised orally, they can then be set as a written sentence-completion exercise.

10 Qu'est-ce que je dois dire?
This activity lends itself to paired work. **A** has a master-card with questions and answers on it. **B** has a card with the jumbled answers only. Each time **A** asks a question, **B** has to find the correct answer from his list. When they have worked through the task, **A** and **B** can exchange cards and repeat the process, even though it will now be a much easier exercise for **A**. The next lesson, it would be profitable to cement the practice and learning done by means of a copy-writing assignment, using the exact written material contained in the previous lesson's master-card.

11 Quelque chose qui commence par ...
This old favourite can have its scope extended by the simple addition of the requirement to give one sentence of information before the group starts guessing.

> e.g. *Je vois quelque chose qui commence par un M.*
> *Les hommes portent cette chose à Twickenham.*
> (le maillot de rugby de Jacques)

Such an addition has the two-fold effect of obliging the animateur to produce more than just the name of the object, and of encouraging the other members of the group to do more than merely call out a list of objects.

Early Sentence Recognition and Copy-Writing

Many of the oral activities discussed above will inevitably have contained elements of written sentence recognition, together with opportunities for copy-writing. The strategies outlined below supplement those earlier suggestions and work on the principle of exploiting material with which the children are already very familiar in its oral form.

12 Trouvez la Phrase!
Apparatus: Master-card for *animateur*, word-wallets or sentence-wallets for the rest of the group.

The animateur reads out sentences from the master-card and the others have to find and construct the sentences from the contents of their wallets. After the very earliest stages, the group then progress to writing out the constructed sentences.

13 A la Fin!
Apparatus: Master-card for *animateur*, word-wallets for the rest of the group.

The *animateur* reads out the sentences from the master-card, minus the last word. The group have to build the whole sentence from their word-wallets and then write out the sentences carefully, once they know they are correct.

In the early stages it is advisable to try to exclude, as far as is possible, any opportunity of incorrect copying. There will be more than enough of this without one's building in extra factors that encourage it—as when one allows whole groups to copy things down without having the complete written material in front of them in its correct form.

14 Racontez-nous l'Histoire!
A small number of objects are placed on the table. The group have to construct the tale of these objects from their sentence- or word-wallets. Once their tale has been quickly checked for errors, they copy the sentences out.

Initiative Activities

As already emphasised, built in to many of the activities offered as suggestions thus far is an implicit element of challenge. One of the problems with teaching a second language is the fact that we tend to restrict it to the mere re-presentation of early experience already acquired, in a new linguistic code. The teacher is faced with the illogic of someone repeatedly quizzing a second party as to his or her name, age, provenance and dressing habits, merely as device to practise a new language, when the information elicited by the questioning is already all too familiar. The difficulty resides in the fact that, in order to use his new language at a later stage in real situations with native speakers, a pupil has to practise with his classmates in unreal situations. Over-practice in unreality is counter-productive. Consequently, a balance has to be struck between unreal, but necessary, practice and a variety of tasks which are meaningful in themselves.

Given such a brief, the following strategies may be of service.

15 Grosse Tête!

Apparatus: Text books and materials from other study areas. Assignments are designed to encourage children to search out information for themselves. In the earlier stages of such tasks, the teacher can make sure that the data required is readily available, or has been very recently discussed (see Fig. 11).

Grosse Tête!

Using your school-books, your eyes and your memory, answer the questions below:

1 Un village romain près de Chollerford, où il y a des lavabos célèbres. (livre d'histoire p. 34)
2 La jeune fille aux cheveux bruns dans la chanson de Stephen Foster.
3 Un port dans le Yorkshire d'où voyage le Capitaine Cook.
4 La ville derrière la colline dans l'affiche près de la porte.
5 Le dernier jeudi de ce mois.
6 Ecrivez en français les noms des trois boissons dans la photo au-dessus du tableau noir.
7 La région où habite notre assistante.
8 Combien de distance est-ce qu'il y a entre Paris et Lyon?
(Maximum de cinq minutes!)

Fig. 11

There is a real urgency, together with a considerable element of enjoyment in activities like the one exampled here. But it also has the advantage of bringing in information from outside the French lesson and once more making French seem less isolated from other parts of the child's work.

As a group activity *Grosse Tête* may be employed as a competition between groups, or for individuals within groups. As a home exercise, often done on a voluntary basis since it does not look too much like homework, it can be made more difficult and less immediate than in Fig. 11.

16 Les Mots Croisés!

At some time or other, most teachers will have had recourse to crosswords with their classes. A useful source is back numbers of educational magazines, from which they can be cut, stuck on to card and used as group exercises.

Apart from the practice they give in testing word-shapes and the application of acquired knowledge and vocabulary, crosswords fulfil another most useful function. For teachers concerned with producing a relaxed, calm and productive classroom atmosphere, the word competitiveness is often anathema, particularly when one is attempting to let children work at their own level within the class, with the less able being made to feel as important as the others. Too much direct competition, with the rank-order assessment it tends to produce for the children to see, would seem to go against all this. Yet, the fact remains that the human animal needs a degree of competition to bring out the best in him. The answer one searches after is the sensitive compromise. Crosswords can provide this, since it is not too difficult to build up a stock of graded *mots croisés* for one's classes. With such a supply class-wide group competitions can be initiated—very hard puzzles for the most able, correspondingly easy ones for the other end of the ability range within the class. The winner is the first group with a stated number of its members (working independently) to finish their puzzles.

Such crossword puzzles, with no written help, are best left until the early stages of copy-writing are finished. For the beginner, it is possible to produce puzzles with the answers scattered around the frame, so there is some assistance (see Fig. 12). Despite the help given, the pupil still has the task of focusing on individual words and their shapes and making decisions as to their meaning. There are few other activities where a child can be found studying the shapes of words, pleasurably, for five or ten minutes at a time.

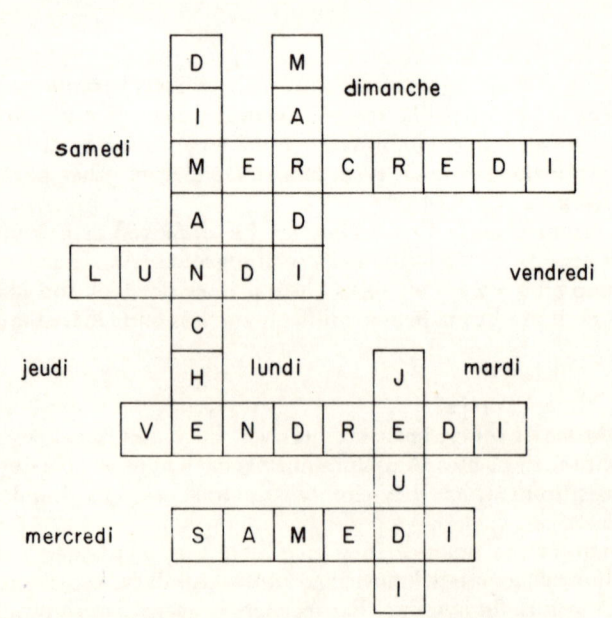

Fig. 12 A beginner's crossword (completed version).

17 Déchiffrez-le-moi!
A companion activity to the last, this type of assignment is useful for drawing attention to and reinforcing recently acquired vocabulary and knowledge. As the pupil's experience of French increases, the task can be made more difficult by presenting the explanations in French.

		Déchiffrez-le-moi!					
	From the clues given in the middle, straighten out the jumbled French words and write them correctly in the blanks on the right hand side.						
1	MECBAMTER	A cheese					
2	HCTELRPOEIE	A means of transport					
3	EREPIR	A boy or a stone					
4	RSPEMI	Needed for driving					
5	ENRVIDDE	A day of the week					
6	CNEIH	You get it mixed up with *chat*					
7	LJITEUL	A month					
8	POETEL	A game					
9	ETNAT	Uncle's wife					
10	NUOLOT	A large navy base					
11	CAHPMGNAE	A sparkling wine					
12	TALUS!	Hullo!					
13	EMBOLOND	A film star					
14	ENGRIER	For storing grain					

Fig. 13 Déchiffrez-le-moi!

Early Reading Strategies

18 Silent Reading
Passages are cut from old copies of course materials (current or abandoned), stuck on card, graded and indexed. The child's reading progress within the group can then be plotted through the year. To check proficiency and effort, specific passages can be accompanied by a set of check-questions in English. With this type of approach, the teacher has

less difficulty in assessing the pupil and, equally, when he or she has to set thirty people working in five different groups, it will be a help to know which passages this lesson's reading group had reached last time; then all they have to do is go to the store and find the next one in sequence.

19 Reading Aloud
One of the major advantages of group work sessions is that they allow opportunities for pupils' reading practice with the teacher on a one-to-one basis, much along the lines of early reading in English. Apart from the opportunity such personal contact gives the teacher for a more accurate appraisal of the pupil's progress, it is a method worth using to combat the general antipathy to class-reading aloud.

20 Écoute-Moi!
This is a dual-purpose paired-activity (cf. p. 55). **A** reads a passage from a card three times, stopping at the end of each paragraph. **B** has another card, with questions in English on the text. After **A** has finished the first reading of the passage, **B** may make an initial rough draft of his or her answers to the questions and is then allowed the second and third reading to finish and polish the assignment. Although a strategy for early reading and comprehension practice, this is another device which is sufficiently flexible for use to the most advanced level, with questions and answers couched in French or English. Basically, **B**'s good comprehension depends upon **A**'s good reading.

Tape Recorder Activities

Because of the relative cheapness of magnetic tape and the ease with which resources can be marshalled for the production of tailor-built programmes, together with the freshness and attraction of different voices, additional taped activities have a distinct role to play in a group-centred work scheme.

21 Au Secours!
Gist reading is an exercise much used of late with lower ability groups, and is gradually gaining common currency as a valid strategy for use with varying age and ability groups. The tape recorder equivalent of gist comprehension is a particularly effective device for maintaining interest and effort and has some relevance to the way in which pupils may have cause to use their French in adult life.

Au Secours! involves the simulated broadcasting on tape of urgent messages, the main points of which must be noted by the person receiving the message, if a potentially disastrous situation is to be saved. In the first example, the pupil is required to get the gist quickly in English (later in French), with the wireless transmitter fading and one minute of broadcasting time left. With a few atmospherics and the sound effect of a failing aeroplane engine, it is striking how much realism can be incorporated into this tape.

> 1.
> *Avion en difficulté ... moteur ne marche pas ... entre Burley et Ilkley ... pilote malade ... beaucoup de brouillard ... pas de parachutes ... appelez l'aéroport de Yeadon et la police ... Répète ...*
>
> 2.
> *Accident de voiture ... dans le bois près de Holmbury St. Mary ... un grand camion ... et une mini ... la mini brûle ... le camion perd beaucoup d'essence ... danger d'un grand feu ... deux morts ... le conducteur du camion sérieusement blessé ... il faut une ambulance ... et la police ... Répète ...*

In both the examples, local British rather than French places have been used, so that the material becomes more real and immediate for the pupils.

22 Communications téléphoniques

A similar activity to the last, *Communications téléphoniques* involves the taking down of specific, important messages. Because the emphasis is on the production of correct, if uncomplicated French, this type of activity is best not introduced before the pupils can be relied upon to reproduce early dictation reasonably correctly. Alternatively, this may well prove a suitable exercise for a high ability group in an early form.

Speed of comprehension is required, as individuals are speaking from a public call box with little small change. The number of times each sentence is repeated depends upon the pupils' capacities and the teacher's aims. As an alternative to what amounts to a disguised, straightforward partial dictation, the children could be allowed to make notes on the call and then rewrite it.

> *Je n'ai pas beaucoup de temps. Ecrivez, s'il vous plaît, ce message pour M. Bewick:*
> *Notre rendez-vous, jeudi 18h ... je ne peux pas venir ... pas de transport ... ma voiture est en panne ... pouvez-vous venir au club de Rugby à Retford, vendredi soir, à 20h 30? ... J'ai l'argent ... Mon numéro de téléphone est Gainsborough 278596.*

The Slide Viewer

The general use of the slide viewer is discussed in Chapter 5. The following activities are examples of how it may be profitably employed in group work.

23 Vocabulary Recognition

Two or three people working with the slide viewer are given four slides. Presented with a minimum target, they are required to write down all the French vocabulary they recognise in the pictures. If a bonus points system is in operation, they are allocated bonus points for any vocabulary noted over the set minimum.

24 Ce qui commence par ...

The group is given half a dozen slides. They have to find and write down all the things that begin with a **c**, or any other suitable letter.

25 Story Composition

Once again, the group is given half a dozen slides, this time with a common theme. The pupils are required to compose a simple story in French from the pictures. In the earlier stages, this would be carried out with the aid of the word or sentence wallet. For more advanced pupils this type of exercise is a neat introduction to CSE and O Level picture composition. The teacher's own slide film is particularly useful with this strategy, as it so often tends to be consistently thematic.

26 Oral Activities (card guided)

Single and series slides are a useful stimulus for question and answer routines, with the pupils working in twos, threes, or the full group, the *animateur* being in possession of a master-card to ensure reasonably relevant and accurate conversation.

Parlons de l'image (Image N° 17)

Animateur, *please ask the following questions and, perhaps, one or two of your own. After each question, you will find the correct answer.*

1 Où cette scène se passe-t-elle? (Au bord de la mer.)
2 Le petit garçon, qu'est-ce qu'il fait avec sa pelle? (Il fait un château.)
3 Et la jeune fille, qu'est-ce qu'elle fait? (Elle écoute son transistor.)
4 Est-ce que le monsieur lit? (Non, il dort.)
5 Le jeune homme à la barbe, que fait-il? (Il plonge dans l'eau.)
6 Combien de gens y a-t-il dans l'image? (Il y en a huit.)
7 Où se trouve la personne qui fume? (Derrière la tente)
8 Faites une liste, tout le groupe, des objets jaunes dans l'image. (une tente, un maillot de bain, une serviette, un canard d'enfant.)
9 Reconnaissez-vous quelqu'un dans l'image? (M. Thrower, dans l'eau!)

Fig. 14 Parlons de l'image

Or less routinely, one may devise activities of the *Vrai ou Faux?* type, using the need for careful observation as a stimulus. For such an exercise, slides would be chosen in which there was sufficient but not excessive evidence to allow the pupil to make a decision on the questions asked. If, for example, the children were employed on a sequence of slides where they were asked to determine whether they were in Britain or France, then the teacher would ensure street scenes with shops displaying a green cross, or red cigar, or with a French policeman discreetly positioned in a corner and with the corresponding British stereotypes. Then the dialogue starts with a statement from the questioner—

> *Cette scène se passe en Angleterre.*
> —*Faux!*
> *Comment le savez-vous?*
> —*Parce qu'il y a un cigare rouge devant la boutique!*
> *Oui, c'est vrai!*

Chapter 4

The Work Card Concept

Amongst the advantages of a French teaching method which is at least partly work card based are the opportunities it provides for a flexibility of approach, personalised learning, incentive work, relief activities, gap and time fillers and help with discipline. Amongst the disadvantages are the time taken by the mental and physical preparation of such materials, their habit of wearing out too quickly and the tendency to use each set of cards as a one-off activity with one group only.

Bearing such points in mind, it is wise to conceive and design work cards for maximum use—both from the point of view of long life and of group suitability.

The need to grade the cards is basic to the method. When dealing with five groupings within a class, the teacher attempts to provide five activities of varying difficulty (see pages 53–55). For group work underpinning a teacher-based classroom method, the grading should be carried out so as to allow some lateral movement, in the sense that Group C could be meaningfully employed on the cards of either Group B or D after completing their own.

Apart from making greater use of cards that have possibly taken some time to prepare and thereby allowing a broader guide for measuring individuals' progress within the class, the lateral conception of work card materials allows for revision or reinforcement practice with individuals from other year groups. For example, a third year secondary pupil having trouble with prepositions after transferring from another school where less French was done may benefit from working with the second year card below.

Implicit in the work card concept is the intention to employ a variety of activities that are well liked and needed by the young learner—items such as memory-tests, multiple-choice and initiative work, and *odd-man-out, spot the mistake!* (not grammatical), as well as more straightforward exercises like overt and disguised copy-writing.

Work cards are particularly useful in providing stimulus and challenge for the young mind. Because it looks like puzzle material found in

THE WORK CARD CONCEPT

Mettez le mot qui manque!

Find the missing place word for each sentence from the list at the bottom and write out the completed sentences.

1 Jeanne sort _____ la maison.
2 L'agent entre _____ le commissariat.
3 La vendeuse se tient _____ le comptoir.
4 Nous allons _____ l'école _____ voiture.
5 Monter _____ un éléphant – c'est haut!
6 Allez _____, s'il vous plaît!
7 Je n'ai pas d'argent _____ moi.

derrière   sur   en   dans   à
de   devant   sur

Fig. 15 Preposition Work Card

children's comics, something as straightforward as the preposition card above will create interest. Also, the fact that such card exercises seem relatively personal and are not contained in a book amongst a welter of other detail (some of it confusing), is of importance.

Simple memory tests are especially well-received and effective. We are very aware of the popularity of activities like *Kim's Game* and there is no doubt that the young adolescent enjoys having his memory teased. One of the considerable advantages of memory test cards (see Fig. 16) is the ease with which they can be conceived as, for instance, a means of revising the last lesson or week's work.

Qu'est-ce qui va?

Which are the correct endings for the sentences below?
Write out the correct sentences in full.

1 Nous voici au bord de _____.   la Garonne/la Loire/la Seine ←——— a
2 Ils sont avec leur _____.   oncle/père/grand-père ←
3 Ce sont nos _____.   cousines/sœurs/tantes ←   b
4 La dame a _____.   craché/crié/chanté ←————— c
5 Le chien a _____.   aboyé/bu/bondi
6 Le contrôleur est _____.   parti/sorti/arrivé
7 Allons vite à _____.   la gare/la maison/Moscou

Fig. 16

The *Qu'est-ce qui va?* card in Fig. 16 was made for use with a course in which there is no written material with the early stages. This is a situation encountered not infrequently. Often, for lack of finance and suitable materials, materials will be used with 13–14 year olds that were designed for first year middle school pupils. In such a case there will be a need for the written word, both for reading and writing purposes. When a school cannot afford new course materials the production of work cards may well be one of the few alternatives available.

While considering the example memory test card, one should note the additional advantage they offer as a supplement to commercial courses, not only from the point of view of materials, but also from that of objectives.

In Fig. 16 the element of multiple-choice has been used to amplify and reinforce general knowledge (**a**), test aural-discrimination (**b**), and add humour (**c**) as well as to test retention of lesson content.

But before examining further practical examples, it is worth considering some points relevant to the production of work cards. With long life a major requirement, it is advisable to use a thicker gauge card if at all possible. Card that is hardly thicker than sugar-paper will last no time. If there is little or no card available in the school, then most teachers will be familiar with the use of card from cereal, shoe and shirt boxes as a substitute.

Assuming a basic supply of card, there then arises the question of coding. On a basis of one card to one pupil, there may be as many as thirty-five (or more) cards in use in the one lesson. From the point of view of distribution and continuation, transfer, etc., this can cause chaos. Consequently the cards need to be colour-coded, or, alternatively, in some way number-coded. In a class of thirty with five groups, there would be a need for five colours (or their alternative), if the groups were based on ability. Five is a sound base, as this is about the number of ability levels a teacher might feel confident of defining within the class. Distribution depends on the way in which the groups have been set up. If the class of thirty has been set into five groups purely on the grounds of ability, then all the members of one particular group would have the same colour card (containing the same assignment). On the other hand, if the pupils are in random groupings, then, for most activities, they would still receive the card assignment relevant to their assessed ability. In other words, the cards would be dispersed around the classroom as they, the children, are dispersed.

The present author's preference for colour-coding (either by the natural shade of the card, or a coloured marking of one's own design) rather than by group-numbering, arises out of the fact that children are much less inclined to try to work out the significance of the colours than that of the numbers. There is also the very practical reason that it is much easier to see who is doing what from a distance, by the colour of the cards.

Before discussing the vital question of who makes the work cards, a further point to promote their long life may be of use. The best materials for covering are the various commercial clear contact polythenes, but they are so expensive as to be unviable. A much cheaper substitute is kitchen-film, but even here, unless significant donations can be obtained from mother's kitchen, the teacher is going to have to restrict its use to those work cards that have to last.

If the teacher takes all the card manufacture upon himself he is unlikely to reach the age of optional retirement. The pupils' cooperation is needed. The thought of personally producing thirty work-cards for one class to be used for perhaps half a lesson at most must be a daunting prospect for any teacher—so daunting in fact that, except for the rare occasion, it is to be dismissed out of hand. But for the teacher to devise the five basic activities and content for the cards is much more feasible. A good class from second year level upwards might be relied upon to copy reasonably accurately from the board. The reliable writers can be selected and set to printing cards from time to time. In itself, the activity is a justifiable exercise in copy-writing. There is, nonetheless, an obvious objection. How can pupils make work-cards containing a surprise or test element for themselves? If, on occasion, we require such cards, then this problem can be resolved by allowing one class to produce material for another. This is much easier in the middle or secondary school than in the primary, since there are more relatively advanced pupils to help. If, on the other hand, there is good liaison between primary and secondary or middle and secondary, then it is possible to find sixth-formers who are prospective teachers and ready to help with production for younger pupils. There is also the Parent-Teachers' Association. It is surprising how many mothers there are who are sufficiently qualified to help with the preparation of materials at home, under the guidance of the teacher.

More immediately, work card production as a homework assignment can be revealingly rewarding. If the children are told just to do a work card, without any preparation, the results are likely to be disastrous, but shown the techniques, they can produce simple ones, which, after correction by the teacher, can be used on their class-mates or another class.

There will be mistakes and crossing-outs, but what the teacher does with the mistakes on the card can underline the usefulness of the card-production exercise for the child as something linguistically valid in its own right, and not merely a piece of justifiable pragmatism on the part of hard-pressed Modern Languages staff. If the cards are gone over with their creators during a group correction session, they can be made to see where they went wrong and either encouraged to do the card again or correct the mistakes with additional small pieces of card, patching over the errors.

By this stage, some colleagues who teach the earliest levels of French will understandably be saying that work cards are a fine idea after the first year or so, but that they cannot be used with almost absolute beginners.

The problem of this early stage is the written word, or lack of it. Therefore, if we are to create work cards, they will have to be based on the spoken word, with, sometimes, perhaps, the simplest of written French to help out. The teacher already implements such a technique with *Loto* cards, a straightforward spoken exercise practising the associations of sounds and numbers. But if *Loto* can be used for early number work, it can so easily be adapted for all manner of vocabulary recognition and recall exercises. Places, objects, toys, animals, fruits can be substituted for the numbers, depending on the availability of a supply of small pictures for the different boards (which will be much larger than the conventional number-boards) or of the finance to buy some of the commercial variety *lotos* available, if that is what one would wish.

In the early months there is also the shopping-list card, as in Fig. 17 below.

Chez Gisèle

Go to the shop, buy the items on this list, work out the cost of each item you have bought and write out the shopping list again with all the prices of the things you have bought and the total:

½ kilo de beurre
1 bouteille de vin
2 bouteilles de limonade
3 kilos de pommes de terre
1 journal
1 cahier

TOTAL _____

Fig. 17 The Shopping List Card

The card above might stimulate protest on several grounds. Firstly, one is going against what has been stated about no written French being seen in the early stages. The question to be asked is, what exactly are the early stages? They would seem to vary from institution to institution. Does the teacher suddenly decide that writing should commence? Or does he introduce it very gradually after just a short while, partly because so many children are becoming genuinely frustrated, since they can write nothing of what they have been hearing for some time? The shopping card is an attempt in this latter direction. The items have been carefully chosen for the frequency with which they have been heard or spoken. The children are familiar with them and negative transfer on an aural-oral level is not likely to be too great a problem. Of course, there will be mistakes in the copy-writing. The reader will be aware of how difficult children find it to write French correctly. On this basis, if the class have had the chance to read out such lists to each other, after practice with the teacher, a gradual start after a short period will appeal to many colleagues far more than the idea of waiting for a year.

Another objection to the card is that the items on the list are rarely found in the same shop, except in a country village and that what is being produced is therefore a somewhat inaccurate representation of the way things are in France. Probably, most teachers would feel that the atmosphere or *ambiance* was there and this was what counted.

To return to the basic technique of producing material to accompany the spoken word, it is worth looking at a category one might call the tape recorder card. Here a somewhat different technique is adopted. The word card before the child has only the instructions printed on it and the bottom two-thirds are left empty. The tape recorder plays a sentence from, say, an *En Avant présentation*, or a Longman's dialogue and, from figurines and cards on the desk, the pupil makes up the sentence, rather in the manner of the display activity on page 103. Thus, if the tape recorder (or teacher) produces *Hélène et Claudine jouent avec la corde à sauter*, the child will place figurines of a skipping rope and Hélène and Claudine suitably disposed on the card to represent what had been heard. From the point of view of construction, tape recorder cards will have to be much larger (something like the front panel of a family-size cornflakes box) to accommodate the visuals.

When, after the first lessons, early sentence recognition is being encouraged, then the scope is immediately widened and work cards can take the form of a card with a picture on it, accompanied by a series of jig-saw sentences that are easily put together. Some element of challenge is ensured, as with the tape recorder cards above, by obliging the pupils to choose from a variety of possibilities in front of them.

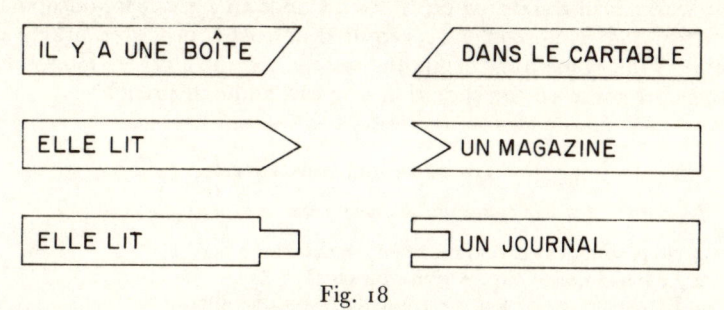

IL Y A UNE BOÎTE	DANS LE CARTABLE
ELLE LIT	UN MAGAZINE
ELLE LIT	UN JOURNAL

Fig. 18

A more complex development of this activity is a sequence of pictures on the work card, with a large number of sentences to be put together and in order. Such an exercise can tend to run away with the space available, and although in the basic jig-saw sentence exercise it will have been possible to blu-tack the sentences to the work-card, any large-scale developments will mean the desk or table top becoming the centre of operations rather than the card itself.

Once the children are reading and working on copy-writing, a considerable amount of potential can be obtained from the combination of card and slide projector—the standard model projector for a teacher-directed exercise and a battery operated viewer for independent group work. A slide is projected (or viewed) and the children have to choose the right sentence from the written material on their card to accompany it. The use to which such a very simple technique may be put is quite extensive. It is very good, for example, for making children look carefully at the singular and plural of verbs. In a slide, is it *Il prend son déjeuner* or *Ils prennent leur déjeuner?* Half a dozen or so slides of this type will encourage attention to the difference between *il* and *ils* and the accompanying change in the verb.

Equally, such a technique can encourage attention to visual detail and provide lively material along the lines of *Spot the deliberate mistake!*, where an erroneous statement is given about the slide shown. *Le car est garé au bord de la mer.*

The pupils are being encouraged to use their wits and the teacher can control the material, because he selects it. Again, a card with eight sentences containing a mistake of detail (but not of language), will repay the effort over and above the enthusiasm it will stimulate. In both the examples just examined, the pupil is being challenged to look very carefully at the written material in relation to what has been seen on the screen or viewer. If the point at issue is not immediately clear it has to be searched for and this has a large effect on language reinforcement.

The slide-card combination can also be effective in promoting initiative work, as in a slide, where, if for instance an activity for vocabulary practice and reinforcement is required, a card is produced asking the pupil, 'Find something beginning with a,b,c,d,e, etc.' or 'How many things are there on the slide that you can name in French?'

Qu'est-ce que vous voyez?

Look at the slide and answer the questions below in French:

1. Nous sommes en France ou en Angleterre?
2. Le bateau, est-ce qu'il arrive ou part?
3. La personne en bleu, c'est une dame ou une fillette?
4. En quelle saison sommes-nous?
5. Combien de personnes y a-t-il dans l'image?
6. Quel est l'objet noir tout près du monsieur?

Fig. 19 Slide Card

THE WORK CARD CONCEPT 51

With a reasonable class of thirteen yearolds, the same slide can be used to combine elements of initiative, challenge and interpretation, with the opportunity to write a little French containing a certain free element, as in Fig. 19.

The map work card is similarly helpful (see Fig. 20), is adaptable, and can be used sufficiently frequently to more than justify its production. If the map is made on a banda or roneo-type master, enough copies can be run off to supply a variety of activities.

With a class who are writing simple French correctly, a start might be made with a direction-finding exercise:

Plan de ville

From the map provided, work out in French THE ROUTE TO THE PLACES STATED.

1 Je suis à la gare, pour aller à la piscine, je ...
2 Je suis au parc, pour aller chez la fleuriste, je ...
3 Je suis sur le pont, pour aller à la gendarmerie, je ...

Fig. 20 Map Work Card

With the addition of a simple grid, the same map can now be used for distance and metre practice, as in Fig. 22.

Graded Work Cards to accompany the Dialogue adaptation from Longman's Audio-Visual French, Stage 2

As outlined in Chapter 2, there is one work card for each ability group. They are reproduced on the following pages in ascending order of difficulty.

The bottom ability group work on *A L'Ordre!*, a card which is fundamentally a disguised copy-writing exercise, with the need to rearrange the sentences in the correct order providing some challenge.

Qu'est ce qui manque? is more demanding linguistically and pitched at a level where the second lowest group could cope. This type of 'Fill in the missing words!' activity is especially useful at such a point in the ability range.

Rafraîchissez-moi la Mémoire! is another exercise in which the pupil is required to complete the sentence, but we have moved a step further on than *Qu'est-ce-qui manque?* with the class we are considering, as the missing element is no longer supplied at the bottom of the card and the pupil is obliged not only to evidence sound-recall, but also to be able to recall written shapes, albeit at a not too demanding level.

The next group are involved on the paired dictation exercises—*Entre Toi et Moi!* There are two cards for this activity for obvious reasons, since

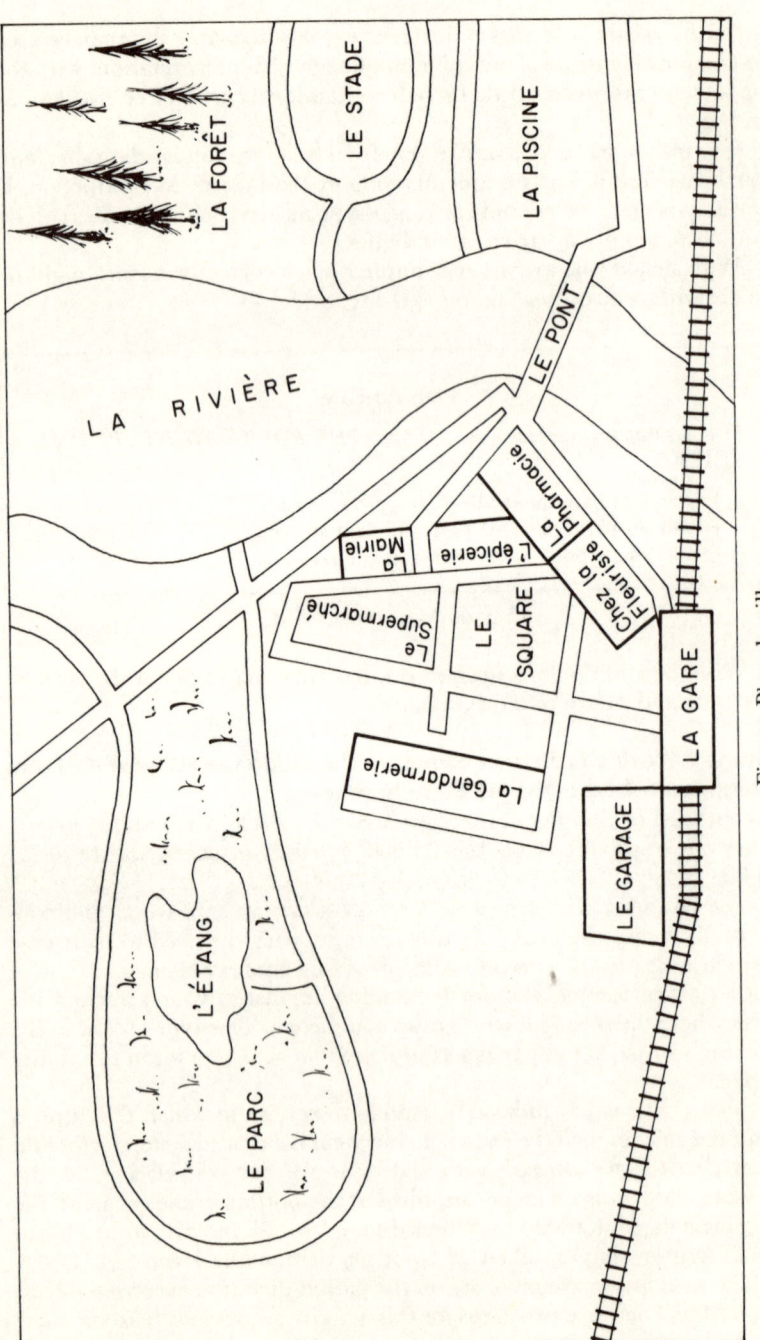

Fig. 21 Plan de ville

THE WORK CARD CONCEPT

Combien de distance y a-t-il?

The grid on the accompanying map is 2 cm: 30 m. With the help of your ruler and on the basis of this information, work out the answers to the questions below:

Combien de distance y a-t-il entre:
1 ... le stade et la rivière?
2 ... l'école et la gare?
3 ... le parc et la mairie?
4 ... le supermarché et la piscine?
5 ... le square et la pharmacie?
6 ... la boulangerie et le pont?
7 ... la mairie et l'étang?

Fig. 22 Distance Work Card

the second reader must have something different to read to his partner, otherwise he will have had an unfair advantage. The idea of pupils giving each other dictation may give some colleagues apoplexy, but in a situation where the children are repeating language with which they have recently become very familiar *a* the risk of consistently bad mispronunciation is reduced and *b* the writer is anyway less likely to be led astray by such errors. In addition, this one-to-one exercise, practised regularly, helps pronunciation considerably, partly for what one might term reasons of mutual responsibility, and partly because the children are being given a chance to do things. There would, however, be unanimous agreement that such dictation is to be kept for the higher-ability groups at this stage.

A l'ordre!

Look at the sentences below and decide which go with which picture. Then write them out with their picture number in the order which they took place.

Voilà ta limonade, Jean-Paul.
Jean-Paul, prends ce panier.
Tu as beaucoup de clients.
Qu'est-ce que vous prenez?
Mettons-le sous la table.
Moi, je prends une glace au chocolat.
Michel, veux-tu prendre quelque chose avec nous?
Tu vas les payer, Hélène, n'est-ce pas?
Hélène et moi, nous prenons un chocolat glacé.

Fig. 23

The last work card (Fig. 28) is clearly the most demanding, requiring some translation. For those who are worried that the very able child often does not get the opportunity to stretch himself, work-cards can be very soothing, since they should clearly afford just that chance. In each of the English sentences, there has been a change made from the original French and some effort over and above that of substitution is required. This particular card starts at picture number seven because similar work has already been done with pictures one to six.

Qu'est-ce qui manque?

The dots in the sentences below mean that something is missing. Find the missing word or words in each sentence from the list at the bottom of the card and write as many of the complete sentences as you can.

Qu'est-ce que vous ... ?
Moi, je prends une ... au chocolat.
Michel, veux-tu prendre ... avec nous?
Mais je ne prends rien ... je travaille.
Attention, ne le ... pas là!
... sous la table.
Michel ne ... pas le voir.
Toi, tu vas les ..., Hélène, n'est-ce pas?

| va | mets | prenez | glace | payer |
| quelque chose | | mettons-le | | quand |

Fig. 24

Rafraîchissez-moi la mémoire

Let's see how good your memory is! The sentences below need finishing. Look at the pictures on your sheet and then try to write out the complete sentences.

7 Qu'est-ce que vous ... ?
  Moi, je prends une glace ...
8 Michel, veux-tu prendre quelque ... ?
  Tu as beaucoup ...
9 Je le mets à côté de ...
  Michel ne va pas ...
10 Toi, tu vas les ...

Fig. 25

THE WORK CARD CONCEPT

Entre toi et moi! A

Read each of the sentences below THREE times, so that your partner can write them down. Do NOT let him or her see this card.

Je prends une glace au chocolat.
Je le mets à côté de ma chaise.
Mais ne l'oublie pas.
Toi, tu vas les payer, Hélène, n'est-ce pas?
Beaucoup de gens prennent une glace.

Fig. 26

Entre toi et moi! B

Read each of the sentences below THREE times, so that your partner can write them down. Do NOT let him or her see this card.

Nous prenons un chocolat glacé.
Michel, veux-tu prendre quelque chose avec nous?
Mettons-le sous la table.
Attention, ne le mets pas là.
Je ne prends rien quand je travaille.

Fig. 27

Below is a series of sentences in English. The number in front of each one indicates the part of your written sheet where there is something similar written in French. See if, with the help of your written sheet you can translate the English sentences into French.

7 I'm going to have a cup of coffee.
8 I don't have anything while I am sleeping.
9 When the weather is bad, many people have a cup of tea.
   Careful, don't put it on the table.
10 Will you take the cake?
   You are going to pay for the coffee, Charles, aren't you?

Fig. 28

Chapter 5

Work Card Activities

Filmstrip Work Cards

Autre véhicule, autres possibilités, to rewrite the French aphorism. But to complete the picture, perhaps one should add *autres difficultés*. Indeed the average teacher is fortunately too wary to expect any medium to be a total panacea. The filmstrip is no exception. In many people's experience it is particularly susceptible to pupil disenchantment at a very early stage, since there is a tendency for the teacher to abnegate responsibility and let the filmstrip do all the work, once there with the blinds drawn and the projector running. But, even if all is not left to the projector, children still seem to lose interest during the filmstrip session.

If the work card can be used to direct interest and to focus attention, again by introducing elements of challenge and the chase, the teacher will be going some way towards solving a basic problem.

	Filtrage!
Image N°	Write the answers to the following questions in French, using complete sentences.
1	Qu'est-ce que la grosse dame portait dans ses mains?
2	Où se trouvaient l'écrin et les bijoux?
4	Qui était la personne derrière le rideau?
5	Combien d'argent y avait-il dans le portefeuille?
6	Est-ce qu'il faisait jour ou nuit dehors?
7	Où se trouvait le coffre-fort?
7	Quelle heure était-il?
8	Qui était la personne moustachue?

Fig. 29

1 Filtrage! (Screen Test)

This activity is based on the well-known children's television quiz. Six to eight frames of the week's filmstrip are worked through in the usual manner, but with the warning that there will be a screen-test immediately after the normal work, requesting specific information relating to each frame.

This particular card was devised for practice in the Imperfect. The same activity was later used with a less advanced group, the Present Tense being substituted for the Imperfect. As we do so much work with different tenses, it is worth remembering for those teaching right through the secondary range that many card activities can be adapted for use up the age-range, by the simple device of changing the basic tense in which they are couched.

To do this is justifiable on two counts. Firstly, it increases the advantage to be won from a card which may have taken some time to devise. Secondly, to allow the pupils to practise new concepts and structures from a basis they will already have been familiar with in the past is to increase the likelihood of effective comprehension and retention. Generally speaking familiarity, as long as it is not overdone, breeds security.

2 Vérifiez-le!

This time the children are given the card to look at before the filmstrip is projected. The lights are put on after each frame, the image removed, and the children allowed to consult the card, which contains a series of

---

Vérifiez-le!

Below is a series of sentences which should fit exactly with what has happened in their pictures. But there MAY be a small mistake in each sentence. Look at each one carefully and write out what you think should be the correct statement.

Pic. No.

1	Le paquet mystérieux est <u>derrière</u> l'étagère.	devant
2	La belle dame porte un tablier <u>rouge.</u>	rouge et jaune
3	L'ascenseur est au <u>premier étage.</u>	rez de chaussée
4	Le liftier cherche le patron.	
5	La vedette écrit <u>l'adresse correcte.</u>	une fausse adresse
6	<u>Frédéric va</u> au secours.	Frédéric et Sylvie vont

Fig. 30 Vérifiez-le!

deliberately wrong statements. It is the pupils' task to correct each statement, on the basis of the way the frame has been developed by the teacher, and to write out the corrected statement. Depending on the teacher's requirements, correction can be made after each frame, or kept until the end of the sequence if it is a really able class which responds to a difficult challenge. In Fig. 30 the mistakes have been underlined by way of illustration, and the corrections put in at the side.

3 Ça finit comment?

After the current filmstrip has been shown and exploited on several occasions, the children are shown the strip on a fresh occasion, only this time they see just the first two thirds of the narrative sequence, plus the commentary. They are then given a card with perhaps a dozen sentences on it and have to choose six in the right order to finish the story correctly.

Ça finit comment?

Now, see if you can finish the story you have just seen by choosing six of the twelve sentences below and putting them in the RIGHT order.

Ils restent sur le bateau.
Le capitaine doit aller au poste de police.
Ces montres-là ne sont pas à moi!
J'ai trouvé les montres.
Roger et Claudine ne peuvent pas aller avec lui.
Comment ça va?
Vous devez venir quand même avec nous au poste de police.
Et pour toi, Claudine, j'ai acheté une montre.
Deux douaniers attendent sur le quai.
Alors, messieurs, montez!
Oui, capitaine, suivez-nous au poste de police.
Je dois examiner votre bateau, capitaine.

Remember: find the LAST SIX sentences IN ORDER to finish the story.

Fig. 31 Ça finit comment?

4 Écrivez la fin vous-même!

This work card activity is an extension and advanced version of the last. Again, the children are given two thirds of the current sequence of filmstrip and commentary, after the material has been well practised. At this stage various possibilities arise according to the age, ability and experience of the groups. With a very able set, the story might now be finished unaided, while another group could be given a vocabulary card to help them and a third, working with loop aerial and headphones, would hear the tape and complete the story from it. Below is an example vocabulary card, aiming to give a group just enough stimulus to do most of the work on their own and to help them with the more difficult lexical items.

Écrivez la fin vous-même!

Now, see if you can write the ending to this episode. Below is some useful vocabulary to help you.

un rendez-vous ... fixer ... de retard ... un mal de ventre ... déconcerté ... il faut ... revient ... personne ...

Fig. 32

5 Truquage!

This is a fun activity which is worth repeating with every filmstrip, since its attraction rarely seems to pall, and for the equally valid reason that it does encourage careful listening and visual identification, especially if one takes the simple precaution of telling the class that *Truquage!* is planned for the next lesson.

The children see the filmstrip with the correct taped material until they are very familiar with it. Then they are presented with the film plus a re-recorded version (produced by the class-teacher and/or assistant or the Teachers' Centre/local languages teachers' group), with six to eight deliberately false sentences substituted amongst the correct material. The children have a work card from which they are required to select the offending utterances. Again, according to ability and experience, this activity can be made more taxing if required by for example obtaining explanations from the children as to why they know an intruding sentence to be wrong. Such a refinement is particularly good for encouraging children to look at the structure and implications of language.

Included below, to show how careful *truquage* can stimulate pupils, is a series of original statements with a series of paired statements in which small changes are of vital significance.

    a   Il a six minutes de retard.
          Il a seize minutes de retard.

    b   Elle a un grand mal de dents.
          Elle a un grand mal de ventre.

    c   Déconcerté, il s'en va.
          Déconcertée, elle s'en va.

d Madeleine est encore là.
Madeleine n'est pas encore là.

e Monsieur du Bellay arrive du bureau de change.
Monsieur du Bellay arrive du bureau de poste.

None of the changes effected in the second sentence of each pair is a large one in terms of its physical size, but in terms of meaning and comprehension, its significance is altogether greater.

a is a standard number change and six to sixteen is perhaps the obvious one to choose. However, units to tens (*trois–trente*) and units to teens, in general (*cinq–quinze*), need similar attention.

b is an internally rhyming noun change (by no means the best example), opportunities for which should be found in any dialogue or narrative sequence.

c the simple change from *il(s)* to *elle(s)* is another profitable strategy to employ in such discrimination exercises as *Truquage!*, since the anglophone often has such difficulty discriminating between *il* and *elle* (in both the singular and plural), that attention drawn in this way to the similarity will help as a correctant.

d the negative substitution is particularly useful, as its addition or omission draws attention to its place in the sentence shape, encouraging the pupil to think about it in a way that is rarely achieved with the written word alone.

e the similar-noun change is especially useful, since its substitution in the sentence can have relatively little effect on the basic message and there is therefore a tendency for it to be easily missed.

Overhead Projector Work Cards

Because of its design, the overhead projector is well worth exploiting for use with shape, and as such can help provide activities for the young early-learner.

6 C'est quoi, la silhouette?

This ploy is an obvious technique for general early oral work, but is also valid for early reading recognition and copy-writing. The children have a work card in front of them containing a list of numbered objects in French. One by one, and in random order, the teacher places the easily recognisable objects listed on the card on the transparency desk and casts the silhouettes. From the card the children have to select the objects in the order they occur, either by writing down their numbers or the actual French.

WORK CARD ACTIVITIES

C'est quoi, la silhouette?

Below is a list of the objects whose shapes you will soon see on the screen. As you see each shape, choose the right object from the list and write it down with the number the teacher calls out.

un stylo	un compas
une clé	une bague
un bic	une bobine
un canif	un bouton
un peigne	une aiguille
une épingle	un trombone

Fig. 33

7 Pour aller...?

This is an extension of the town-map group work activity on page 51, and, once again, an adaptation of a familiar overhead projector strategy. A map transparency is projected and the group have to fulfil the tasks specified on their cards, as in Fig. 34. The exercise is a flexible one and it is easy to devise half a dozen different cards for a group, merely by altering the starting points of the individuals trying to find their way, as below. In the earlier stages, basic expressions of direction can be included at the bottom of the card as an *aide-mémoire*. Alternatively, these expressions can be numbered, with the individual merely required to choose the correct ones, in order, and write the numbers down.

Pour aller ...?

Write out* the routes required by Jacques and Céline, using the expressions at the bottom to help you:

Jacques:
Je suis à la gare ... Pour aller au square, s'il vous plaît?
Céline:
Je suis à la piscine ... Pour aller au vignoble, s'il vous plaît?

Allez tout droit, tournez à gauche/à droite, première à droite, deuxième à gauche, juste devant, prenez le raccourci, passez devant, montez la colline, descendez la rue.

---

* For oral activity substitute 'Tell the group ...'

Fig. 34

7 Ce n'est plus là!

Ce n'est plus là! is an overhead projector variation on *Kim's Game*, taking advantage of the scope offered by overlay transparencies. The group are given a work card with a list of all the vocabulary they are about to see on the screen. Then they are shown a composite, projected picture, consisting of one base and one overlay transparency for thirty seconds or a minute. Next, the teacher or *animateur* removes the overlay and the children have to write down what has disappeared from the picture. To make this exercise more demanding, more vocabulary could be given on the card than was actually contained in the original picture. By way of exploitation this basic activity could be practised a second time, only without the card on this occasion, if the pupils were felt able to write out the material from memory without too many mistakes.

Ce n'est plus là!

The objects that will disappear are all in this list. Look at it quietly for a minute before you see the picture on the screen. Then listen carefully to the teacher's instructions.

des ciseaux	une punaise	un tablier	une manche
une fleur	une lime	une bouteille de vin	un livre
un bonbon	un clou	une charrette	une livre
une charrue	un tracteur	un manche	uene roue
			une rue

Fig. 35

9 Avant

Because of the overhead projector's facility for superimposition, it is an excellent device for verb tense work, since, by the use of colour-coded overlays, the teacher can create a visual impression of tense changes, quickly and clearly.

In the activity for which the card in Fig. 36 was designed, the structure *avant de* is being used with a group of fourteen year olds to practise the *Passé Composé*. In each sentence, which has already been practised until the children are familiar with it, the *avant de* action is drawn in bright colours on the transparency and the previous action done in black on the overlay, on the basis that black/colour gives some of the psychological feel of previous/more immediate action.

Radio Broadcasts

Many of us have tended to make relatively little use of the B B C radio broadcasts for young beginners in French due to timetable pressures.

The teacher has often felt unable to give more than twenty to thirty minutes a week to the radio material and has therefore decided either not to participate at all, or to restrict the class to a once-through listen to the broadcast as an extra and by way of variation.

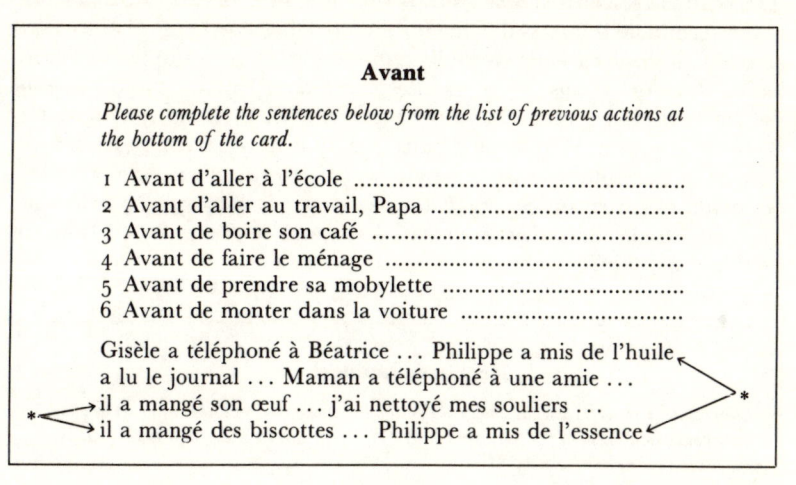

Avant

Please complete the sentences below from the list of previous actions at the bottom of the card.

1 Avant d'aller à l'école ....
2 Avant d'aller au travail, Papa ....
3 Avant de boire son café ....
4 Avant de faire le ménage ....
5 Avant de prendre sa mobylette ....
6 Avant de monter dans la voiture ....

Gisèle a téléphoné à Béatrice ... Philippe a mis de l'huile
a lu le journal ... Maman a téléphoné à une amie ...
*→ il a mangé son œuf ... j'ai nettoyé mes souliers ...
→ il a mangé des biscottes ... Philippe a mis de l'essence ←

* Two distractors

Fig. 36

Such concern to complete the syllabus is very natural, but it is possible to make much wider use of schools' broadcasts as a basis for language work by adapting them to work card activities. Before looking at the suggestions below, it is worth noting that the recent beginners' series, *Salut les jeunes!*, apart from being excellent material in its own right, contains many very worthwhile suggestions for productive and relevant activities that lend themselves to group and work card sessions.

The basic work card assignments that can be adapted to a broadcast are:

1 English comprehension
2 French short answer
3 French standard answer
4 Multiple choice
5 Gap-filling
6 Transcription
7 Exploded text

and, indeed, most of the other exercises encountered are a variation on one or more of the above. With the exception of 2 and 7, the categories listed have either received considerable attention elsewhere in this manual, or do not require special examples at this stage. Let us look, then, at French short answer and exploded text card techniques, together with the ubiquitous multiple-choice test.

10 French Short Answer Techniques

As has already been discussed, one of the difficulties of early written work in the second language is the inevitability of a high percentage of written errors if questions are not carefully chosen. Fig. 37 is a sample work card listing those questions that guarantee short, sharp answers at the beginner level. The questions have been given with their completions, for easier illustration. With such a pattern of questions relating to a broadcast, it is possible to ensure single word or phrase answers and the opportunity for relatively correct answering, working on the principle that the longer the answer elicited the more mistakes it will almost certainly contain.

Réponses rapides!

Starting on your left, ask the group the following questions, one at a time. When you have gone right through the list, start with a different person and complete this list five times.

De quelle couleur est ...?	Bleu
Combien de ...?	Trois
Où habite ...?	A Dax
Comment s'appelle ...?	Maurice
Quel âge a ...?	Onze ans
Quand ...?	En été
A quelle heure ...?	A 7h.30
Comment est ...?	Grand et bête
Où est ...?	En Suisse

(*One point for each correct answer.*)

Fig. 37

When one studies Fig. 37, it is illuminating to realise how many of the question forms employed in the early lessons can be made to almost insist on short answers. It is worth noting that, once the teacher starts using interrogatives like *est-ce que?* or *Que* ...? he encourages *oui* or *non*, or leaves himself open to a variety of problems at this early stage.

11 The Exploded Text

The exploded text is particularly useful for providing dialogue (and reading) practice for the relative beginner. After the class have attained to a reasonable familiarity with the original broadcast, they, or a small group, are presented with an exploded version of the dialogue and a script card, as below, and are required to play the role omitted on the gapped version of the tape. To ensure the individual child is not left floundering without any help, various things can be done to the tape. For general support and correction the tape can be made so that the pupil is faced with alternating original and exploded versions of the dialogues, e.g. orig./exp./orig./exp.

A major difficulty encountered with this type of exercise is the pupils' natural hesitancy, or alternatively their over-anticipation, resulting either in their missing the intended gap, or coming in too quickly on top of the preceding voice. To overcome such problems, either a standard long gap of three times the length of the original utterance is built in, or there is a soft cue-bell at the beginning of the explosion. With this type of device, one will usually find that the pupils cope quite adequately with exploded texts.

Exploded dialogues are most effectively done in the laboratory situation, when the children can record their own voices on the pupil track, but they remain a worthwhile exercise even in the normal classroom, be it working in the looped aerial situation, in a small group with a tape recorder in the centre on output only, or, sparingly, as a whole class activity.

Radio Nous!

Below is your part in the radio programme, with dots in between to show when other people are talking. First of all you will hear the complete conversation, then it will be repeated, but this time leaving gaps for you to speak. To help you come in at the right time, you will hear a faint ping when it is your turn to say something.

... Je ne l'ai pas vu, moi! ... Mais, ça doit être sérieux. Un espion, peut-être! ... Non, je ne blague pas. Francine a disparu.... J'ai trouvé ses souliers sur la plage.... Ecoutez, vous l'entendez? Il y a quelqu'un derrière le mur.... Maman va me voir! ... D'accord, je vais le faire.... Mais ça va être difficile.... Allons, ce sont les cambrioleurs d'hier!

Fig. 38

12 Multiple-choice

Multiple-choice work is particularly suited to the radio since it offers challenge and reinforcement at the same time, and gives a concrete element to something which, through being wire-less, runs the risk of being lost in the air somewhere between the apparatus and the pupil, if he or she is not allowed frequent straightforward exercises which help to tie the spoken work down to the written. The specimen card in Fig. 39 is an amalgam, to show how multiple-choice can direct the ear.

Faites votre choix!

Answer the questions below by ringing the letter of the answer you think is right.

* 1 Alain joue avec
  - *a* une bille
  - *b* une balle
  - *c* un ballon

* 2 Bérénice est
  - *a* la sœur de Bertrand
  - *b* le frère de Bertrand
  - *c* la sœur de Jean-Yves

* 3 M. Claudet est
  - *a* détective
  - *b* gendarme
  - *c* motard

* 4 Le premier visiteur est
  - *a* Américain
  - *b* Russe
  - *c* Anglais

* 5 Dans l'histoire, nous sommes
  - *a* à la campagne
  - *b* au bord d'une rivière
  - *c* au bord de la mer

* 6 Daniel donne
  - *a* 4½
  - *b* 45
  - *c* 85

  francs au garçon de café

* 7
  - *a* Cécile et Didier vont à la péniche
  - *b* Cécile va à la péniche
  - *c* Didier va à la péniche

* 8 Une natte est
  - *a* une sorte de tapis
  - *b* une mouche
  - *c* ce qu'on fait dans sa cravate

Fig. 39

*Each category provides a different test objective, as set out in the following list.

1. Pure single-sound discrimination.
2. Relationship awareness.
3. Sub-classification differentiation (background information and culture-based).
4. Voice and accent awareness.
5. Receptivity to sound cues.
6. Deduction from build-up of information.
7. Singular and plural person action-awareness.
8. Definition.

A test of this nature serves the excellent purpose of pinpointing individual pupils' areas of comprehension difficulty. For example, someone who is continually having trouble with questions of the category 7 type may find the concept of the change of verb-form for the change from singular to plural persons and vice versa difficult to understand. Similarly, a pupil who is continually experiencing problems with type 1 questions will reveal himself as having special difficulties with sound recognition, and remedial work might be undertaken.

Language Laboratory Work Cards

The honeymoon with the language laboratory is long since over and the majority will have found their partnership with this particular machine to be a difficult marriage, not necessarily merely because of its inherent weaknesses, but because, like many a human being on whom such finance and maintenance has been lavished, too much has been expected of it. Frequently, it has been installed in a school without any consideration being given to the provision of laboratory teaching materials, and it has been expected to function as a panacea. Frequently, too, because of its cost and its size, one may have been expected to use it all the time to justify its costly presence.

Conversation téléphonique

Please take part A. In the early stages of this conversation, part B will be taken by the tape. Next lesson, you will be working with another member of the class playing B. Before you start practising, you will hear the full conversation three times on tape. Now, listen to further instructions from the teacher.

A Allô, c'est toi, Michel?
B Non, Michel n'est pas là.
A Qui est à l'appareil, s'il vous plaît?
B C'est son père.
A Alors M. Simon, où puis-je le contacter?
B Il est chez Barrault. Attendez, j'ai le numéro de téléphone. Ne quittez pas ... Allô?
A Je suis toujours là, M. Simon.
B Eh bien, M. Barrault, c'est CONDORCET 9316.
A CONDORCET 9316. Merci bien, M. Simon. Au revoir.

Fig. 40

In the past then, lack of specific materials and over-use with individual classes have led to the laboratory being regarded as a white elephant. Now, with some specific courses and course materials available, we have reached a saner position and realise that sparing and well-directed use of this adjunct can be a positive benefit. Particularly so when it is remembered that the language laboratory, by its very concept, lends itself to a variety of effective, interesting and potentially lively learning activities and not merely to pattern-drills.

13 Paired Link-Ups
If the laboratory has the facility for pair work, then a whole gamut of activities is available. Apart from adaptations of many of the foregoing suggestions, the link-up can be used for telephone conversations, ordinary dialogues, guessing games, dictation, initiative exercises and role-playing; all of which can be card-controlled. The telephone conversation in Fig. 40 can be practised with the card and gradually learnt by heart, with the rider that pupils be allowed to add what extra detail they like.

This is a particularly helpful stage in encouraging future ad-libbed conversations.

14 Role-Playing
As we know, one of the disadvantages of whole-class role-playing and dialogue practice in the normal classroom situation is the distraction frequently caused by everyone talking at once about different topics. Because of the dynamics of the lab and the way the headphones and tape-recorder encourage quieter responses, such activities can be pursued relatively easily in the booth situation. Exploded dialogue work like that in Fig. 41 would be a basic exercise, but there is even more scope

---

Dialogue

Having practised the dialogue already, you are now quite familiar with it. See if you can play your role in the gaps on the tape with little help this time. Below are the last few words of each speaker except yourself. Now listen to the master track for further instructions.

PR	.... des contrebandiers.	PR	.... la route.
CL	.... Roger?	CH	.... moi.
RO	....	PR	.... la clé.
CL	.... la route!	PR	.... Roger.
CL	.... travaux.	CH	.... suite.
RO	....	RO	....
CL	.... maintenant?	PR	.... au vent.
RO	....	RO	....
PR	.... de voiture.	PR	.... le voit.
CL	.... de voiture.	CH	.... t'échapper.
RO	....	RO	....

Fig. 41

with exploded conversations, if there are a filmstrip projector and screen set up in the lab, so that the pupil can be supplied with a synchronised visual stimulus. With the role-playing card below, the pupil takes the role of the character who has been exploded-out, after the class are already well familiar with the material on the film and tape. (Roles can be given as a home-learning exercise and the pupil's part later left out of a copy of the dialogue text, with the requirement that he or she should write it in).

15 Filmstrip Commentaries

Filmstrip commentaries are a straightforward and flexible exercise, which can be made to cater for the most and the least able. After the current filmstrip and tape have been well worked through, the pupils are presented with the film and are required to tape a commentary. Each frame is projected for long enough for the slowest to cope, more details being expected from the most able, and the class can be given as much or as little help as is felt necessary, by the addition (or omission) of graded 'help-cards', of the type illustrated in Fig. 42. With a class containing a great discrepancy in ability levels the same standard and volume of commentary will not be expected. By way of written practice, the top groups can be got to write down their commentaries after they have recorded them, and allowed to polish their work for a further recording on another occasion. A useful incentive for classes of fairly uniform

---

Faites le commentaire!

Imagine you are in a film studio. The sequence you are about to see needs a spoken commentary. Next to each frame number you will find some vocabulary to help your memory.* Now, listen to the console for further instructions.

Frame No.
1. la mi-temps ... se sont reposés ...
2. un sandwich ... faim ... soif ...
3. dernière minute ... pour égaliser
4. le ballon ... les poteaux ... gagné ... gardé ... souvenir
5. revenus ... bonne journée ... rapporté ... méchant
6. au garage ... curieux ...
7. hésité ... le sous-sol
8. l'arrière ... sacrebleu! ... tout expliquer ...

* Re-done as a written exercise next lesson

Fig. 42

ability is the knowledge that the commentaries into which the most effort has been put will be transferred to a master-tape, broadcast to the class or used with next year's group.

Filmstrip commentaries are also excellent revision strategies, as a film from several months back can easily be projected at very short notice and a commentary requested. No one will need reminding that there will be a considerable fall-off in the content of the commentary of most pupils in comparison with their original efforts, but regular revision of this sort will be found to increase long-term retention.

16 Imitations

This exercise will be regarded by some colleagues as heretical, but for those who are willing to try it, it makes good use both of the laboratory's capacities and the younger learner's natural imitative ability. Local assistants record a tape, containing a series of statements, with a high emotional charge of some description, and the appropriate changes in intonational patterns. The pupil's task is to repeat each of the sentences and capture the emotional flavour and intonation. For this task he is encouraged into releasing his inhibitions and his main aim is to sound convincing. The card accompanying the exercise makes it clear that something specific is being transmitted with each change in intonational pattern, and that this is a pleasurable activity, since it is essential the individual pupil should be as relaxed as possible.

Les Voix des gens F*

In a few minutes you will hear the sentences below on tape. Each change in the way the voice sounds, shows a change from anger to fear, annoyance, enjoyment, happiness etc. When you start recording, try to sound just like the voices. Now listen to the console for further instructions.

> Donnez-le moi.
> J'ai une peur bleue.
> Je suis heureux!
> Il a fait ça!
> Je trouve le clown ridicule.
> Mais, on n'a pas téléphoné.
> Tiens, tu as raison!
> Allez, vous pouvez le faire.
> C'est drôle, ça!
> Voyons, mon vieux, calme-toi!

---

* F – female voice. Separate sequences male and female voices, with no cross-imitation.

Fig. 43

Practical, Job-Centred and General Interest cards

The themes in this section are chosen for their ability to interest and even motivate problematical pupils in the thirteen to fifteen age-range (see pp. 91–93).

17 The Car Card
The card is one of a series of activities, including simple technical translation, model and performance comparisons, research into car and company histories, and basic diagram translation which provide a cohesive programme for car-orientated pupils in their last year of French before dropping it. Except by special request, luxury models are omitted from the scheme, so there will be some semblance of reality for the pupils in the lower socio-economic groupings.

18 The Cookery Card
Cookery provides an excellent opportunity for the French teacher to work in conjunction with the Cookery or Home Economics Department. Working consistently through a series of simple dishes over the year, the pupil can acquire a respectable fund of basic *cuisine* language.

19 The Fashion Card
Fashion activities offer similar stimulus and a surprisingly wide accretion of language. If the type of fashions worked upon are matched with the pupils' social backgrounds and preferences, the project is likely to be a lengthy success.

20 The Commerce Card
Commerce is another area in which in integrated approach with other study areas can be developed. Fig. 47 is one of a series of assignments developed after discussion with a school commerce department and local firms.

21 The Football Card
It is not too difficult to build up a collection of football activities like that in Fig. 48, through the cooperation of the *assistant(e)*, Teachers' Centre and native French colleagues, in procuring the necessary newspaper and magazine articles. If these are not available however, the *assistant(e)* may be persuaded, *à la rigueur*, to provide simple translations of English reports on French or Franco–English football.

Car Card 4

Look at the advert below and answer the questions in English:

> Avec la Simca 1100 vous avez une amie sûre. L'amie du conducteur qui apprécie la sûreté de sa tenue de route (traction avant et suspension à quatre roues indépendantes), ses accélérations, son freinage à double circuit.
> C'est aussi l'amie des passagers avec ses sièges confortables. Grâce à sa banquette arrière rabattable, vous triplerez le volume du coffre.

1. Give the make and model of the car.
2. What is the first thing the driver appreciates about the car?
3. Is it front or rear wheel drive?
4. What kind of suspension is it?
5. And the brakes?
6. What should passengers like about the car?
7. What is special about the back seat?
8. How much is the boot size increased?
9. How does today's car compare with the R12 we looked at in Card 3?

Fig. 44

Recette du jour 14

Salade Française

Below is the first part of next week's recipe. Translate it into your French recipe notebook. When you have all finished, we will go over it, to make sure there are no mistakes:

Faites chauffer de l'eau dans la petite casserole et quand elle bout, plongez les deux œufs, à l'aide d'une cuiller, dans l'eau bouillante. Faites cuire 9 minutes. Puis, retirez les œufs et plongez-les dans une bassine d'eau froide, pour les refroidir.

Après cela lavez les feuilles de laitue et séchez-les dans du papier absorbant.

Ensuite, ouvrez la boîte de haricots verts, rincez-les doucement à l'eau froide dans une passoire. Coupez-les en morceaux de 1–2 cm.

Fig. 45

Fashion Card 10

A la Mode!

Please answer in English the questions below the magazine extract. The photographs in which the outfits are described are No's. 24, 25, 26.

> a *Page de gauche:*
> *Pour lui, veste en alpaga et cachemire à col rond, chemise en flanelle quadrillée, pantalon de flanelle beige (300F, 120F et 150F chez Boutiques Bel Homme).*
>
> b *Pour elle, cardigan ceinturé en laine rayée (180F Modothèque), jupe en velours côtelé (180F Simon Richas, Boulevard St. Michel), bonnet chez Mario, écharpe au Printemps.)*
>
> c *Page de droite:*
> *Pour lui un gilet sans manches en gros tricot jacquard avec une longue écharpe assortie (270F chez Elvire). Pour elle, un manteau long en gros tricot rayé, longue écharpe et bonnet assortis en vente (400F environ, G. Lafayette).*

a
1 Describe the model's jacket.
2 What are his trousers made of and how much do they cost in English money?

b
3 Describe the model's cardigan.
4 What is her skirt made of?
5 Which of the three shops mentioned would you guess to be the most and least exclusive?

c
6 What is the man wearing?
7 Give the meaning of the words *'longue écharpe et bonnet assortis en vente'*.
8 What does the initial 'G' in the last line represent?
9 How many well-known department stores are mentioned in the extract? Name them.

Fig. 46

Commerce Card 22

Réponse urgente!

Below is a short letter your boss has brought into the office. He needs to have as accurate answers as possible to the questions that follow it.

A l'attention de:
M. P. Davies,
Service d'Exportation.

"Chic Hose",
Bettaspun Mills,
Bradford.

Objet:
N/commande 47/78   Strasbourg, le 12.9.78.

Monsieur,

Nous vous remercions de votre correspondance du 17 juillet et du 11 août et de votre facture n° K 49751 relative au règlement des 20,000 paires de bas que vous nous avez livrées par suite de notre commande citée ci-dessus.

Malheureusement, nous avons été étonnés de constater que tous les bas sont en nylon. Si vous relisez notre commande du 3 juillet, vous verrez* que nous avons bien spécifié '15,000 paires en nylon, 5,000 paires en laine'.

Nous vous prions dans l'intérêt de nos bonnes relations de régler cette erreur le plus tôt possible.

Veuillez agréer, Monsieur, nos salutations distinguées.

X. MACHIN-TRUC
CHEF D'IMPORTATIONS,
MODOBAS.

1 *Is the letter a re-order, complaint or what?*
2 *Is the tone friendly, matter-of-fact, pleasant or unpleasant?*
3 *Does it require urgent action? If so, why?*
4 *What is the status of the person writing it?*
5 *What do the figures 15,000 and 5,000 refer to?*
6 *Why is the date '3 juillet' there?*
7 *What is he asking me to do in the last main para?*

(*vous verrez = *you will see*)

Fig. 47

Football Card 14
MICHEL PLATINI

Read the article below carefully and then answer the questions:

> *Pour la rencontre France–Bulgarie, mercredi, 300 000 personnes ont tenté d'obtenir un bout de banquette au Parc des Princes (50 000 places). La France est folle, folle de ballon, folle de Platini, le premier véritable «grand» du football français depuis Kopa. La saga Platini – cet homme qui s'amuse sur les stades – c'est aussi celle du réveil du foot français. Les joueurs français sont 1 300 000 aujourd'hui. Parmi eux, un joueur d'exception, un homme au tournant de sa vie: Michel Platini.*

1 What is the capacity of the *Parc des Princes*?
2 How many people did not manage to get a ticket?
3 Who is *Platini*?
4 What, according to the article, is happening to French football?
5 How many people play football in France?
6 What do the last three lines tell us about Platini?

(If you have forgotten some of the vocabulary in the article ask for the sport vocabulary cards.)

Fig. 48

Chapter 6

The Preparation and Use of Visual and Taped Materials

Ideas for making visual materials to supplement what is or is not available in commercial courses tend to be restricted to picture cards and flashcards, when work cards (perhaps containing a picture element), mobiles, photos, photographic slides, overhead projector transparencies and maps may be wider in their applications and, in certain cases, easier to prepare.

But whatever visual materials teachers intend to produce, most share at some time or another common feelings of inadequacy because of what they see as a lack of personal artistic ability. We are bad at drawing, therefore we cannot produce effective visuals. Fortunately, this is by no means the case and careful attention to preparational method will allow the creation of materials of a relatively professional standard.

1 Basic Picture and Flash Cards

If the teacher does not trust his own line-drawing, or is loth to spend time making traces and then applying them to card, then a simple solution is the magazine cut-out. The difficulty here is that, although he may have a good idea for a picture, the exact scene he requires is rarely available in the magazines and catalogues to hand. Consequently, if he is going to make a number of cut-outs for card, he would be advised to keep a folder of likely pictures from which he can draw when the need arises. This will cut down considerably the likelihood of finding nothing suitable for a particular topic. Frequently, too, he will find that an almost usable picture does not contain exactly what is needed. In these circumstances, there is the tendency to neglect the obvious device of imposing an overlay cut-out on to the base picture to give the complete visual required.

One reason for the often less than professional appearance of such visuals is the adhesive that has been used. Generally speaking, the wetter and stickier it is in its original state, the wetter and stickier it is going to be on the card to which it has been transferred with its picture. Dry glues of the *Pritt* variety are particularly good for avoiding such problems and producing a non-stained finish.

If, however, the intention is to cover the visual with a protective plastic, or kitchen-film, then the adhesive can be dispensed with, since the protective will hold the picture(s) in the correct position, provided it is carefully applied.

Apart from their protective qualities, plastic and kitchen-films, artists' fixative spray and light coats of polyurethane clear varnish all tend to give the visual an acceptably professional finish.

Very often if a picture is left unadorned it may not be at its most effective, and felt-pen highlighting, through the use of circles, crosses, ticks, underlining, matchstick-figures, depending on the reaction required, will draw attention to specific features required.

A means of varying and sustaining the visual impact of the picture card is to offer a change from the basic square frame by the simple method of cutting the border to follow the contours of the picture. This is pleasing to the eye and is, in fact, easier to produce than a perfectly square frame.

When picture cards are required to have some sort of labelling or accompanying sentences, a clear and interesting highlighting technique is to produce the written stimulus on a separate piece of card and then to mount it on the original. This will give an attractive three-dimensional feel to the visual, but, more important, will literally allow the written message to stand out.

Alternatively, captions can be given extra impact by the use of the anonymous letter technique, i.e. words and letters cut out from various magazines and newspapers. This is a particularly good device for obliging the children to read what is on the card, since the odd shape of the words seems to compel the eye.

The concept of attractiveness in picture cards is an important one, and not merely from the point of pleasing the children. It goes without saying that the more attractive the card, the more potential it has as a learning-aid. But there are limits. It should not, for example, be made so full of detail that the child is swamped by the amount of visual information it contains.

Similarly, beautifully executed drawings of, for example, a series of single animals, are limited in their application relative to the amount of time spent on their production. With such visuals, the technique of picture transposition is useful for allowing single-idea visuals a degree of flexibility. The technique is a straightforward one and merely involves the imposition of a small (group work) picture-card on to a much larger class flashcard, by means of some velcro or blu-tack, to extend the message given by the original card, e.g. a large, early-stage flashcard of *un chat* is presented to the class with a smaller visual of *un poisson* attached to it. This compound message now allows scope for structure practice (oral and written):

> *Voilà un chat et un poisson!*
> *Le chat mange un poisson.*
> *Le chat aime le poisson.*
> *Le poisson n'aime pas le chat!*
> *Le chat est plus grand que le poisson.*
> *Le poisson est moins grand que le chat.*

A further element to remember in both the construction and use of visual materials is the humour content. As we know, a little comedy will rescue many a classroom situation and if some humour can be built into the visuals produced, the teacher will not only be adding something valuable to courses that are often very short on this important ingredient, he will be making it easier for the child to learn. A funny visual is more likely to be remembered than a neutral one, and so is the accompanying French. Consequently, when there is a choice of pictures representing a vocabulary item or structure to be exploited, one would do well to choose the funnier picture. Similarly, if we have found that, despite our feelings of ineptness, the children have responded well to our blackboard matchstick figures, we should not be loth to incorporate them in the picture-cards we make.

Photos

Some of the uses to which photographs can be put have already been discussed in Chapters 4 and 5. Mounted on card and if possible covered with a protective film, they make excellent picture cards, though they are generally too small for teacher-based flashcard work. If, however, they are merely mounted without highlighting and without having picked out the detail we wish to emphasise, we fall into the particular trap offered by the photograph. The camera lens takes in all the detail in its field of vision, whereas the teacher will need to select for reasons of pupil inexperience and lack of vocabulary and structure. So the child's attention must be directed, even if it means cutting away part of the photograph, or blanking out. Incidentally, the same point will often apply to magazine cut-outs.

Photographic Slides

Again, these are an aid, facets of which are examined elsewhere. They have immediate manufacturing advantages in that, if the facilities are available, they take much less time to prepare than card visuals; they allow ease of highlighting, and can be projected to a very large size.

Generally speaking, if the local secondary school does not have the facilities, then either the adviser, teachers' centre organiser or a helpful camera club can find the means for the teacher to make slide film of his visuals. For composite or single-detail pictures, once the cameras and enlarger are available, normal commercial 35mm film can be used to produce film with relative simplicity. When the visuals have been stuck lightly to a white border paper, it is possible to go ahead and photograph, with a quite professional finish. As for highlighting, one covers the section of the picture that is not required with a piece of white card, or focuses in on the specific detail required.

Slide-film is a particular boon for supplementing the visual material in a text-book based course which has little or no ancillary materials. Publishers will often give written permission on request for the photographing of text-book illustrations, provided the school has already bought the books and the film is for use within the school.

Outside of the book or magazine illustration, slide-film has the positive excellence that it can be completely manufactured by the teacher to suit exactly his or her own ends. Scenes relating to the work done in units of the course being followed can be simulated in school and the film taken. This has the advantage over impersonal pictures that it includes familiar people clearly enjoying themselves. A suspicious-looking figure, wearing sunglasses, seated in a chair with a bottle of Dubonnet on the table next to him, and reading Paris Match, is the basis of a slide from which much can be spun.

Overhead Projector Materials

These can take the form of individual transparencies (often framed), or of items on a continuous roll of acetate film, and they have the advantages of long life, flexibility, and ease and speed of production.

A basic O.P. visual takes much less time to produce than a conventional card one, for the simple reason that one can trace immediately on to the acetate film from the original illustration. This facility provides the opportunity to reproduce illustrative material with which the children are already familiar, thus increasing the likelihood of language recognition from text-book to projection. Equally it can promote effective written work by helping towards the easy production of pictorial stimuli for class (or group) exercises. If a clear, direct picture can be drawn at the top of the transparency and then a related written assignment produced below, this will prove particularly useful for directing the pupil's efforts.

An appreciable number of teachers work on the basis of producing special (framed) transparencies for lessons that require thorough preparation and exploitation, and of using the general purpose acetate-roll for material and points that arise during the lesson. Provided one has one's own roll which can be taken off should another teacher require the projector, this technique has the great advantage over board-work that one can store the roll. This means that any material drawn or written *à l'improviste* in the lesson and found very effective, can be kept and repeated with another class or year group when required. When the teacher has to write at length for class dissemination and for grammatical explanations with older pupils, he may be grateful to the overhead projector for permitting him to avoid tedious re-copying and allowing a most useful record of past work.

Overlay-transparencies are almost as easy to produce as basic individual or roll transparencies. If a start is made with the base picture and the overlay clipped on top before it is drawn or written upon, the positioning of the added material will be exactly right. In this way, provided a white card or piece of paper is placed under the bottom acetate film, and good quality O.P. pens used, the teacher will be able to see what he is producing clearly enough to manufacture half a dozen or more overlays, one on top of the other.

Offset-Copier Visuals

If the local Teachers' Centre or other resources centre has an offset-copier, or the adviser has access to one, a lot of time can be saved, provided a high standard of illustration reproduction is not required. It is not suitable if detailed and relatively minute examination of the picture in question is necessary with, for example, a worksheet activity.

The worksheet is produced very simply by the typing or writing in of the written material on the lower section of a blank sheet of paper and leaving the section at the top for the picture(s) to be copied (assuming permission has been given by the publishers). The illustration, which must not be larger than the space allocated, is sent with the master sheet and the copier completes the process, at approximately the same cost as normal roneoing.

The offset-copier can often come to the rescue when there are very few copies left of a previously successful worksheet, containing written material, plus some laboriously drawn pictures. If the copy is a clear one, the offset-machine will cope with it and produce a new batch, sometimes of better quality than the original. Of course, this pertains equally well to the copying of original banda-materials.

Projector-Prints

Projector-prints are a relative luxury, as they can be time-consuming and are best suited to general classroom display, although they do make excellent large-size flashcards.

The slide of which a copy is required is projected on to a sheet of card, acting as a screen, and one traces round the image cast with the appropriate felt-pens. Depending on the complexity of the original scene, the process can take five minutes or an hour, but the final product is a piece of passable art-work. The technique allows the reproduction of slides of French scenes or topical figures which have a germ of authenticity about them, or, equally, a 'rogue's gallery' of the classroom inhabitants for description work.

Taped Materials

Most colleagues feel the need, at some time or other, to supplement commercial materials with their own tape recordings. The following elementary pointers may be useful.

The Classroom
Apart from the recording of in-lesson material and activities, the classroom is probably the worst place for direct microphone recording, since the size of the room and the large area covered by glass combine to produce low quality acoustics. This can be somewhat mitigated by the drawing of curtains and the use of standard sound-proofing, but, in our age of economies, such provision is likely to be exceptional. In general, the smaller the room the better, provided the walls are not so thin that next door's noise comes in (and ours goes out). Additionally, if our recording room is fairly small, we can do something to soundproof it without laying ourselves open to major expense by the use of old curtains, egg trays and boxes and a gradually built-up stock of polystyrene tiles.

Ideally, the tape recorder should be easily transferable from one room to the next, or to the other half of the split-site campus. It should provide straightforward operation and a facility for recording in combination with another source, such as a second tape recorder, wireless or record player.

Leader-Tapes
Before starting recording, it is advisable to decide upon a consistent leader-tape system. These come in different colours, all of which stand out sharply from the mid to dark brown of the magnetic tape. If a colour code is adopted for use with the leaders and they are spliced into the magnetic tape (in approximately foot lengths), they will give a clear indication as to what follows when they are seen passing through the tape-heads. The coding system devised might be similar to:
    green = personal insert; red = oral activity to follow; blue = gapped passage to follow; yellow = keep for next lesson;

or alternatively:

> blue = recorded dialogue; green = original material from commercial tape; red = class exercise; yellow = French song.

Splicing

The need to splice sometimes accounts for a reluctance to adapt tapes. Some of the excellent splicing kits available can look sufficiently complicated to repel the unmechanical teacher.

Yet the job of splicing is very simple done manually, with a proprietary splicing-tape, or, *à la rigueur*, a normal adhesive tape.

Nowadays, because so many early French courses are being radically revised, with the disappearance of large amounts of original material, it is worth the time taken to splice out part of an old tape and bring it a little up to date. This will save not only money, but minutes of hunting around the original tape in class to avoid passages no longer considered necessary—especially if one has forgotten to mark the footage on the box.

Similarly, one should remember that as well as splicing-out with original materials, there is splicing-in. If sometimes we feel that a section of a tape is well worth doing, but that as it stands it is a little bald and requires some introduction or explanation, the insertion of a short addition may be most profitable.

Teacher and Assistant-made tapes

Direct microphone recordings

Direct microphone is a term used to indicate those recordings made by an external microphone, as opposed to source to source recordings, in which a connecting lead between the tape recorder and another source (tape recorder, wireless, record player) switches the recording to the internal microphone.

Assuming a recording room in which the conditions, if not ideal, are at least acceptable, a routine similar to that below will provide a basis of method.

Recording speeds

$3\frac{3}{4}$ i.p.s.: for normal dialogues, reading passages and conversation.
$7\frac{1}{2}$ i.p.s.: for songs and other musical activities, and very difficult advanced comprehension passages.
$1\frac{7}{8}$ i.p.s.: for lengthy readings only.

Speed of utterance

Two thirds of the native speed with first to third year beginners. Then progressive increase at own discretion. When one is reading towards normal speed, comprehension problems may be eased by extending the natural pauses between the sentences.

Repetition gaps
Depending on level of ability of class and complexity of material, twice or three times the length of the native utterance (spoken quietly under breath).

Voice composition
With early classes and their equal ratios of boy and girl pupils, an equal balance between male and female recorded voices. Where single-sex classes exist, recorded voices should match the sex of the class. This way, learners get sufficient chance to practise the correct intonational patterns for their sex.

Voice variation
With reading and comprehension passages, there is a tendency for the reader to fall into a monotonic, institutional form of expression. It is essential for voices to convey a range of emotions.

Microphone
Standard reading position, i.e. as far away from the average of the speakers' mouths as the newspaper is held by someone with normal reading-vision. The nearer one approaches beyond this point, the more the predominantly nasal pattern of vowels is distorted. If a microphone stand is not available, quality is improved by placing the mike in an elevated cardboard or polystyrene box that has been cotton-wool or tissue-proofed. If some voices are used regularly, one should note their optimum microphone recording level and sitting position for future operations.

Sound effects
In all but the most straightforward of comprehension passages, the insertion of sound effects will prove an excellent aid to comprehension. From the point of view of the recording personnel, as well as being fun to do, they give additional texture to the programme under production.

Signature tunes
Apart from the fact that these may add an element of topicality or background to the recording, they help the pupil to settle in and out of the recording and give a cheerful, lively start to the proceedings. Equally, they can be used as a method of coding by the teacher, as a kind of sound leader-tape, snatches of the signature tune being interspersed at strategic points. Such tunes do not, of course, have to be French. A current hit, provided it has sufficient melody to it, can be recorded in an instrumental version, and new French words written for it.

Before concluding this brief look at some aspects of the manufacture of taped materials, let us return to the cassette recorder. Inevitably, families are acquiring more cassette recorders and fewer open-reel and, if we wish children to do work with tapes at home, then, clearly, it is to the cassette that we must look, especially when we remember that its major disadvantages lie mainly in the direction of teacher-manufacture and teacher classroom-use. As an instrument for individual and small group work in second language learning, its qualities far outweigh its defects. With it, one can provide:

a) *A compact tape-library*, from which pupils can take tapes home to work on individual assignments (provided master-copies are kept, in case of erasure).

b) *Teaching-point tapes*, to help with specific, individual difficulties, such as reading, accent and intonation problems, grammar-point explanations, background information. If a group of teachers and assistants are prepared to co-operate in producing a bank of such material, it means the children have access to extra and relevant personal tuition at home, offering a chance of recovery to those behind for whatever reason other than total lack of ability, and the opportunity for the more able to move on at a greater speed and do justice to themselves.

A scheme such as the one posited here depends upon a good copying service being available, either through the Teachers' Centre, local training institution, or the adviser.

c) *Radio programmes and excerpts* are simplicity itself to record if the school has access to a cassette recorder with an in-built radio. Lately, these have come down in price and are very cheap, considering the scope they offer.

Recordings of direct programmes from France would have the restricted target of the Sixth Form, but the task of committing to tape the BBC junior and middle-range series would be so simplified in those schools without a copying or technician service, that many more children would receive the benefits of the Corporation's latest, well-received courses. All this would occur because the cassette radio-recorder records from itself, so to speak, without any need for compatible machines, complex wiring schemes and correct jackplugs.

A major advantage of such a facility is the fact that a school initiating, say, an early French group, but without the money to buy expensive equipment, could record the current BBC junior French series with the minimum of effort and the cost restricted to a few ordinary cassette tapes, together with the necessary pamphlets.

Chapter 7

General Classroom and Lesson Procedure

'I don't have the confidence!' 'I wish I knew what I was doing!' These are common sentiments expressed by many French teachers at sometime or other. 'And then there's the noise! We can't have them all talking at once without the other teachers complaining!' How often have colleagues commiserated with one another along these lines in the staff-room, the Teachers' Centre or on an organised course? Confidence, method, classroom-discipline. At times these three seem to desert us when we don our French-teaching identities. Yet, there are more successful moments. There are teachers who are generally happy with their French-teaching. We all of us have encountered at least a few who produce consistently excellent lessons. Behind that excellence, there has frequently been a willingness to experiment and, almost always, the application and adaptation of classroom techniques that have proved sound in other areas of the curriculum.

The majority of teachers believe that good teaching has to come from a positive, purposeful classroom atmosphere, where the children can develop their interest, have some idea of what is expected of them and from which the chaos of indiscipline and its bedfellow, lack of organisation, has been excluded. There is much that can be done within the sphere of general classroom procedure to achieve such an atmosphere. Not everything suggested below will work, not all of it will be right for every teacher and every class. But, if the evidence of a wide spread of experienced and not so experienced teachers has any relevance, there will be something of use to all in an attempt to develop confidence, method and classroom atmosphere.

Classroom Instructions

The optimum situation is one in which all commands are issued in French, immediately understood and acted upon and replied to in correct and apposite French. The reality is known to be very different.

Frequently, general classroom procedure is carried out almost entirely in English with occasional recourse to *'Taisez-vous!'* and *'Levez-la main!'*. It is all very well to be condescending towards the teacher who uses only English and to dismiss him or her by saying they are not trying. The reality may well be a harassed, well-meaning colleague with a full time-table, little guidance as to method and who spends much time transporting materials, flannelgraphs, easels and hardware from classroom to classroom. It is little wonder they sometimes take the line of least resistance and resort to a high English content in their French lessons.

But even the most harassed amongst us can gradually reduce the amount of the mother-tongue introduced into lessons, with a carefully phased introduction of commands and responses in French. In addition to those who have been too pressured, there will be a considerable number of teachers who deliberately refrain from issuing commands and requests in French because they believe and know it to confuse the children. For both groups of teachers, there is the same potential solution. Many have found it difficult or impossible to conduct classroom business in French, because too much has been attempted at once. Armed with helpful lists of classroom instructions, one may have adopted the blanket approach and swamped the children in a welter of *directives* which has brought confusion to both the teacher and the taught.

The classroom language should be graduated and lead from the more essential and straightforward to expressions which, although useful, are less of a priority. Incidentally, when the children reach the copy-writing stage, the classroom phraseology with which they are very familiar is an excellent source of written material particularly when children are demanding to write what they are saying.

Thus, the key to the situation is graduated or phased introduction. Expressions like 'Ferme(z) la porte!', 'Je voudrais un(e) volontaire' will figure early *a* because they refer to a frequently recurring situation *b* because the action or situation to which they refer is clear to the child. If we are discussing keys to situations, this last point is of importance. Much of the difficulty experienced with classroom language stems from the fact that the child does not understand either what he or she is being asked to do or what the reply should be. Frequently, neither the command nor the normal reply is understood.

To avoid, or at least counteract this situation, there are several things that can be done to improve method and its end-production. Firstly, the premise of a gradual, phased introduction of classroom commands is accepted. Secondly, the teacher makes sure the child knows what is being said. If, for example, a child is told *'Allume!'* confirmation as to what has been asked may be given initially in English. After the first two or three occasions the explanation may well be modified if the child is in difficulty with the command, by the teacher asking someone else to perform the action and illustrating without the use of English. If the class is a low ability one, experiencing more than average difficulty, it may be felt advisable to ask in French for the action to be done, then in English, then in French again and to continue such a procedure with newly introduced *directives* until the children are familiar with them. As a means of reinforcement one can arrange revision sessions of five minutes within the lesson, devoted to classroom phrase-work along the lines of '*Jacques dit....*' or where the children take over as teacher and issue what requests they can remember, or according to a mimed stimulus.

In the early stages, particularly in the first year of primary French, there are those who feel it is a mistake to expect the child to repeat its side of the command formula. If a pupil has been told '*tire les rideaux*', it is often compounding a difficult situation to expect or even insist upon an elicited '*Je tire les rideaux.*' If one gradually obtains this reply, this may be all to the good. Many would argue, though, that to insist on the reply, '*Je tire les rideaux*' is to create an artificiality of speech that may be as responsible for a child's confusion as its lack of linguistic tools. In other words, puzzlement at this strange need to repeat a command, when normally the child merely gets on with doing what is required, may considerably inhibit learning. Clearly, many *directives* require some form of verbal reply, but if a happy balance can be achieved where no reply is verbally necessary, then this may help considerably the smooth running of the lesson. When one begins to concentrate on the *je*, *tu* and *il/elle* forms with the basic verb, this may be the time to dwell on the command verb. Even here, rather than to insist on the straight verbal repetition of what has been done by the person after it has been done, it is better to work from '*Qu'est-ce que je fais/tu fais/il/elle fait?*', as this is likely to have much more meaning for the children.

Problems within the class are also created when, with the best of intentions, the teacher embarks upon a complicated explanation of a new procedure in French and ends up with a class of children who have not understood. This happens particularly frequently when new games are being explained. As a general rule, a quick, clear explanation in English will avoid confusion and save much time. Again, an explanation first in English, then in French and briefly again in English, with the mother-tongue being gradually phased out over the next few occasions the activity is embarked upon, will help towards a greater and more effective use of French in the classroom, but even the most thorough and able teacher will not achieve a hundred per cent success all of the time. Here, as in so many areas of school French, group work has a role to play (see Ch. 1–3).

The Register in French

The register in French has the advantage for the pupils of being an activity which they can relate very easily to the normal English procedure. The danger for the teacher of '*Maintenant, le registre en français*' lies in the fact that it becomes a stereo-typed, not to say sterile activity if it is restricted to *'présent'* and *'absent'*. If the teacher can gradually introduce a variety of alternatives to 'absent', such as *'malade, en vacances, chez le médecin (docteur), à la clinique, avec le proviseur, en retard, dans la cour'* etc., then the register can have some meaning at the beginning of the lesson.

Specific Responsibilities

Because of the concentration on spoken language in the early stages of school French, the teacher who normally lacks confidence in his or her ability to control the class is likely to find the problems exacerbated when confronted by a class requiring French teaching. In fact, many experienced teachers with good classroom control and an effective but relaxed manner find in the initial stages (and sometimes later) that they are *losing* their French classes. As is discussed in another chapter, this is partly caused by what we might call *excessive single pupil-teacher oral contact* within the lesson, where the majority of the class are often required to sit and listen to the conversation between the teacher and one child or a very few pupils over the major part of the lesson. As in other areas, group work has a role to play in ameliorating this situation but, leaving it aside for the moment, one may find other factors within the classroom procedure which can be put to work against the loss of control.

Pupil Involvement in Class Routine

A majority of teachers feel that they spend too much of their time carrying materials from one room to another, only to have to spend between ten and twenty-five per cent of the lesson preparing flannelgraphs, searching for figurines, tapes, charts and setting up tape recorders and projectors. With complicated time-tabling in the secondary and middle schools, and even in the primary school nowadays, we are fast reaching the position where it is impossible to arrive in a room in advance, or even to set up in one's own room in advance; either because there is already a teacher in the room or the time before the lesson is just not available. We are familiar with the syndrome in which the teacher has to pitch straight into a French lesson on returning from the football field or the swimming pool, or gym in the hall, or music.

In such a situation it is essential that the pupils be trained to take their part in the preparation, setting up and running of the lesson.

In a teacher-based lesson containing the 'excessive single pupil-teacher oral contact' mentioned above, the extra involvement of pupils who were responsible for the visual-aids and hardware would be a bonus, just for the fact that several more people would be doing something other than simply listening or sitting uninvolved with the occasional short patch of speech. Yet, children organising the materials and operating the machines often have an effect on the lesson which is further-reaching than the original intention of taking a little load from the teacher.

Freed of the responsibility for making everything work within an electrically and flash-card controlled lesson, the teacher can actually think about the content of his lesson and whether he is handling the teaching-point as effectively as he might. Class-control becomes more satisfactory when the teacher is less concerned with finding the tapes, the right order of figurines and the solution to the problem of how to balance the teacher's book in one hand, a flashcard in the other and turn on and switch off tape-recorder and projector at one and the same time. An exaggerated picture? Of course, for the most part, that is. Almost all of us can remember nightmare lessons where software, hardware and teacher have become inextricably intertwined.

Thus one accepts the logic of some pupil control over material and machine, but it must be well organised. A two minute explanation at the beginning, middle or towards the end of the lesson, as to how the various buttons on the tape-recorder work will create rather than solve problems. Two or three break-times given up to train willing helpers and lunch-time session (during wet weather for example) showing exactly how machines function, allowing the pupils to run through the procedure themselves, and showing them how to arrange and tidy figurines, flash cards, etc. will soon repay the time spent.

It is advisable to try to extend the volunteer system so that most people in the class can be responsible for something on a rotation basis. A suggested allocation might work thus:

Projector: three to four operators to work on a rota or sometimes in pairs. In cases of absence, the next person on the list to take over.
Tape-Recorder: as per the projector.
Flannelgraph: two operators to work alternately. The same procedure as above in case of absence.
Poster-Easel: as per the flannelgraph.
Figurines: three people to be responsible alternately for the arrangement and correct lesson provision.
Posters: two people to be responsible alternately for the arrangement and correct lesson provision.
Other Visual Aids: three people to be responsible alternately for the arrangement and correct lesson provision.
Co-ordinators: two people to be responsible alternately for the smooth running of the above, to check on absences, etc.

The above division of labour which is flexible and to which extra areas of responsibility can easily be added can be expanded to take in virtually the whole class at the teacher's discretion.

Such a scheme requires organisation, but once running ought to continue smoothly. If a pupil has to know what tapes, figurines etc. have to be used for a particular lesson, then the simplest method is to pin up a sheet, similar to Fig. 49, on the Friday before the week for which it is intended.

	CLASS	PROJ	T-R	F/GRAPH	EASEL	VIS. AIDS
MON 1	2 NORTH	JM 14	DR 33	SA	PL 72 – 80	RN 17,49,117
2	1 SOUTH	RP/3	FL 6	MN	GG L6 – 22	SB 12,35,57
3				etc.		
4						
5						
TUE 1						
2						

Fig. 49 Weekly equipment rota

The above rota is designed for the specialist or semi-specialist, but a less complicated rota for the primary school teacher with one or two classes for French is equally useful.

The initials in each lesson-box refer to the pupil of the day and the number or numbers next to the initials indicate which filmstrip, tape, figurines, posters and additional visual aids are required. This means, of course, that everything has to be catalogued and numbered, so that *a* a pupil can find the materials (when a teacher is in the room) without great difficulty and without referring back to the teacher all the time and *b* there is a minimum loss of materials, since something lost can be at least partly traced back to the last person(s) responsible for its availability. The same people who prepare the materials for the lesson are responsible for their return at the end of the class.

Time spent at the beginning of the year or term numbering and cataloguing every single piece of material to be used is usually well-rewarded and it need not be the teacher who does it all. One or two lunch-times and a few half-hours after school with a volunteer group will soon have the materials straight for the year. Once the scheme is in operation, it works well. Although there are always lessons during the year when the wrong tape has been put out, a visual has gone absent without leave or no one has noticed that a duty pupil is absent; much less time will be wasted than in the situation where the teacher sets up everything for every lesson.

One point the less experienced teacher, I am sure, will not mind being mentioned. For those children who are operating the tape recorder and projector, make sure you plug in and switch on at the socket yourself. This may mean a couple of minutes lost, when a keen pupil might have been running the tape through on the recorder for you before you arrive, but better a little time lost than a nasty accident when teacher was out of the room. Additionally, projector lamps are less likely to blow when the teacher is in the room. Most of us would agree that children do tend to be more careful when we are there.

The scheme assumes that every teacher of French within the school will have their own set of materials basic to the commercial course in use, be they flannel or magnetic figurines and a set of posters, or flashcards or wall-charts. At the moment, figurines are still cheap enough to make it worth indenting for a personal set. If funds are low, then posters, etc. may continue to have to be shared. Another advantage of the scheme is that planning a week or a fortnight ahead, the French teachers in the school can have a reasonable idea of each other's requirements and avoid clashes of material use. This happens frequently when two teachers are involved with parallel groups, but if cross-borrowing has to occur, then it can be allowed for on the rota.

It is worth trying to match pupils' talents to the tasks for which they will be responsible. Some boys, for example, are more technically minded and proficient than their teacher, some are not. It is sound procedure to direct the less well-coordinated to areas of responsibility other than the tape recorder and the projector.

This last point also relates to the question of class control. The non-technical teacher can have his or her world brightened by the boy or girl who is conversant with the tape recorder and projector. Tools which once ruled now serve and those furtive pauses, developing into prolonged silences and grimaces which were so disruptive of the classroom atmosphere can disappear for ever.

On the very positive side, such pupil-teacher cooperation as results from months of working together can lead to a productive intimacy similar to that often found in, for example, the art class, where children will be seen working and discussing away, during their break-times and lunch-hours out of interest. When the criticism is often levelled that the French is quite out of step with the general ethos of the school, this is worth bearing in mind.

Difficult Schools and Children

There are many schools and pupils for whom much of what has been suggested in this and other chapters will be impossible. Difficult schools and difficult, not to say problem, children require strategies which may often seem to have reneged upon higher teaching aims. In schools with a severe discipline problem, the majority of the discussion on classroom display in the next chapter will seem irrelevant, since any material put on the walls would not survive from one day to the next.

Similarly, the pupil's motivation to do French in such schools will often be even lower than for other subjects, since it seems to have no relevance to future jobs and prospects. In high and secondary schools of the type under discussion, morale may be low both amongst the children, because of depressingly deprived backgrounds, and amongst the staff, since all the potentially available brighter children have been creamed off elsewhere.

A situation is then likely to be encountered in which French would appear to have no meaning whatsoever for young people who are most unlikely to have the slightest contact with France and the French once their schooldays are over. In this same situation the staff may well be expected to enter their pupils for traditional CSE and 'O' Level examinations, which they have no chance of passing. Along the way, seventy to ninety per cent of those learning French at the beginning of the high or comprehensive school will have dropped or opted out.

Faced with this not unusual pattern, it is tempting for the teacher, too, to opt out and feel satisfied if behaviour and atmosphere have been maintained at a tolerable level. Yet, there are strategies that can be employed to expand pupils' horizons and provide activities relevant to future occupations.

Opinion is generally unanimous that the most difficult age-group at high school level are the 13+–15+ children. With the middle streams, with whom most problems seem to occur, a bad discipline situation can be ameliorated by grouping within the class on a special basis—sex, ability, interest, activity, behaviour—according to teacher preference. In the latter category, some teachers find that relatively troublesome young adolescents grouped together may be diverted into activities less conducive to the destruction of the lesson. Implicit in such a move by the teacher may often be the decision to provide an alternative curriculum for troublemakers who will be dropping the subject within a year. This is not to say, however, that total victory has been conceded and that, to all intents and purposes, troublesome adolescents have been allowed to drop French while a year is still to be served in the classroom.

The example work cards at the end of Chapter 5 show that it is possible to devise alternative activities for the fourteen year old that are interesting, relevant and of some use for the future, be the pupil obstreperous, or simply more limited in his or her abilities and prospects.

For these children, who are to be non-examinees, a programme of work can be constructed so that it concentrates on more practical and job-centred activities. For the boys, it would contain assignments such as the learning of automobile vocabulary (from *Paris Match* car adverts), or the reading and understanding of simple adverts, bills, factory packing-slips and assembly instructions. Local factories can be very helpful by providing examples of the latter items with which they have had to deal. Of even more help to the teacher than this simple provision is the proof it offers to the pupils that a little French might after all be of some use.

For the girls, commerce, fashion and *cuisine*-centred activities (see pages 72–4) will provide a very wide base. There is the advantage with these particular study areas of joint projects and linked work with the school's Commerce and Home Economics departments. The ensuing cooperation, in itself, is a major factor in improving the attitude of girls who are not interested in French.

Objections may be levelled against this type of integrated approach on the grounds that it presents a grossly diluted diet of French. Frequently, the reverse may be true. Broadly average children who previously showed no inclination to wrestle with the complexities of tense construction will still be largely apathetic in this direction, but they will often accrete vocabulary and expression with some enthusiasm in their areas of new-found interest.

Internal certificates of achievement can be produced within the school to provide tangible proof of proficiency in factory, commercial and *cuisine* French, albeit at a modest level. This device can be rendered even more effective as a motivator if links can be established with local factories, shops and offices.

In the oral context, survival situations are likely to promote derision or apathy with difficult and disadvantaged pupils, partly because of on the one hand the opportunity they offer for noise, and on the other, the simple fact that most children from a low socio-economic background are most unlikely to ever set foot in France. The adolescent passion for football and pop-music can be used here to persuade the pupil that he or she might at some time go to France for a European Cup match or an important pop-concert. Once a degree of credibility is established, useful work is possible.

Passing reference has been made to children entered for CSE examinations, in which they have little chance of success. The teacher has more room for manœuvre with such pupils than is often realised, if he is prepared to opt for a Mode-II or Mode-III syllabus to be designed either in conjunction with a small group of other schools, or totally independently. The syllabus does not have to follow the relatively traditional lines of many Mode-I standard Board examinations and could be based on the types of activities and study areas just discussed, if the teacher is prepared to accept a top marking threshold of Grade three, or Grade two, commensurate with the top ability of the pupils with whom he has to deal.

Chapter 8

Classroom Display and Decoration

Not a few teachers feel diffident when discussing classroom display and even more insecure when it actually comes to decorating the French classroom or the French section of their classroom. Many others produce a classroom which is bright, lively, well-ordered and gives the impression that here is a room in which things are happening. Many more, probably the largest category, fall into the middle position, where when moved they can produce exciting and meaningful decoration, but lack the time and the decorative skill to be continually concerned about the state of their walls, floor and ceiling. In a job which has grown progressively more difficult and potentially stressful over the last ten to fifteen years, this is all too understandable, particularly when calls are being made on the average teacher from all directions and fatigue is the common state.

Classroom display entails time, work and application, and for it to be successful, given the pressure on the teacher, it must be designed to be easily changed and adapted, relatively self-servicing, and susceptible to pupil-involvement.

Also, it is generally accepted that display material that is left up until it yellows, or just for sufficient weeks for it to become ignored, is counter-productive. Consequently, material must be changed reasonably often.

Let us assume that the walls, ceiling, cupboards and windows are bare. The room can now be divided into activity areas and interest corners.

It is a matter of personal choice whether to decorate all at once, having collected the necessary materials for each and every section, or to take one section at a time.

Whichever approach is adopted, the one essential material and element is the pupils themselves. If the teacher decides to do most of the work himself—both the collection of materials and the decorating—then both teacher and pupil will have missed an opportunity. Part of the reason for the new-look room is that the children should feel it to be theirs. An equally important part of its *raison d'être* is its effectiveness as a teaching vehicle. Apart from saving valuable time and energy, the enthusiastic involvement of the children in the decoration of their classroom has an important effect on what happens in the classroom. If the room has been built-up and maintained by the boys and girls themselves it is less likely to be damaged or ignored by them. The teacher too can benefit considerably from working closely with his pupils and can often get to know them better in these relatively relaxed construction and decoration sessions. An encouraging experience of colleagues and of the present author is the relative ease and frequency with which volunteers present themselves for workshops. Classroom control can be mightily improved by a little purposeful cooperation during such a session.

It is well and fine to talk, as in the preceding paragraph, of 'enthusiastic involvement'. One has a right to be suspicious of textbook exhortations along such lines. Suggestions of this type will seem fatuous to say the least, when a teacher has been trying without any marked success to elicit interest and enthusiasm for language teaching materials which may well fall far short of arousing his own interest and enthusiasm let alone those of the children. Such a state of affairs is one of the prime reasons for a new approach to classroom display, since a well set-up and well stocked teaching room provides so many opportunities to adapt, extemporise and move outside of and away from the standard commercial materials with which one is provided.

The Classroom Division

Divide the room space up into the activity areas and interest corners you find personally suitable (see page 98). You may wish to have a very clear demarcation line between one area or topic and another, or, alternatively, have the display changing gradually from one section to another. If you prefer the obvious demarcation, then there are various ways of achieving this effect. Assuming that you have decided to start from the door and work your way round the walls and that your first area/corner will be a *coin géographique*, you can isolate and underline that section by providing a backing of a distinctive coloured crêpe or sugar paper. Alternatively, the section could be backed by blue, white and red, instead of a single colour, to produce a *tricoleur* effect. The next section would then be backed by a contrasting colour, or left with no backing. If further underlining of boundaries is required or if backing paper is in short supply, then there are a variety of proprietary coloured adhesive but non-damaging tapes which may be used. In fact, a strip of coloured tape stuck vertically from the top of the wall to the bottom is often quite sufficient.

Most teachers who are keen on display divide their room into sections because it makes for logical ordering and helps to avoid clutter, hotchpotch and confusion. And this not merely from the point of view of physical tidiness. Materials that are clearly set out are more likely to be clearly received by the child's mind. In addition, the children know where to look for what, and you and they have a better idea as to what are the weaknesses and strengths of your joint display.

Ensure at the planning or at least at the decoration stage that a fair percentage of the display materials is detachable so that individual objects may be used by your class as lesson materials, and topic and project aids. Some of the display must also be easily removable for you to use during the teacher-based part of your lesson. Such use will, of course, often be intentional and planned in advance, but it may equally often be impromptu. A well-stocked classroom can save the teacher in those moments when he runs dry, mislays the correct visual or is searching for a clear comparison.

One does not stop at the walls. Many activity areas and interest corners may well overflow on to a table, small cupboard, desk, etc. placed in front of them. An L-shaped structure—wall and supporting projecting surface in front—gives considerable flexibility to the particular display area. Primarily, the logic of the surfaces simplifies display. With a wall and some form of table, one has a vertical surface for poster, picture, frieze, collage, and graph display and a horizontal surface for realien.

One can go to town on the ceiling, so to speak. Its use as a teaching demonstration area by many teachers will be relatively infrequent. If it is then seen primarily as a decoration area, which can do much to create atmosphere in the classroom, then a variety of possibilities emerge. Pupils and teacher will have spent much time, energy and inspiration producing purposeful areas with a certain specificity and teachability content. With the ceiling, here is the opportunity to relax. If the ceiling can convey enthusiasm, humour, even a streak of zaniness, it will do much to create ambiance in the classroom before the lesson even starts.

A primary colleague in Carlisle had a beautiful, luridly phosphorescent skeleton, made of cardboard one hastens to add, hanging and swinging from the ceiling. Of dubious teachability perhaps, although he assured us that *Belphégor* was very useful for teaching the parts of the body. But the children loved him. There was no particular Frenchness about his bones or his skull and as a teaching aid he was limited, but he gave the room atmosphere and a touch of lugubrious class.

No-one would suggest that the ceiling should be a mass of suspended skeletons and similar macabre creations, but one such invention, fulfilling possibly the role of the class mascot, provides a humour point and does much to help the children feel the room is theirs.

On a more serious note, but still remembering the ceiling as a fun area, this surface may be used most effectively for grouped mobiles. For example, a project on transport could result in a series of card, paper, or papier-mâché models—cars, vans, lorries, aeroplanes, ships, balloons and space modules. These can be easily transferred to most ceilings with the aid of some string and drawing-pins (possibly supported by blu-tack). Logically grouped in a corner or spread over the whole surface, they may be used to reinforce and in some cases extend the transport vocabulary given in the early stages of many courses. Such a display is also most useful for early number work in French and for practising basic structure such as *Combien de . . . y a-t-il? Où est . . . devant/derrière* . . . etc. If the teacher goes as far as to indicate north, south, east and west on the ceiling, then the latter's usefulness is obviously extended. *Où est/se trouve?* can now be widened to take in geographical points as well as locations in relation to other objects. Armed with shopping-lists for vehicles and or whatever mobiles are on the ceiling, journeys can be made to the four points of the compass orally and eventually in writing, and if one is brave enough to continue as far as the ultimate extension of this device and produce a map of France covering the ceiling, then the potential is considerable.

There will be those amongst us who will understandably not feel drawn to producing a ceiling-map, but, there are other things besides mobile groupings and full-scale maps of France that can be achieved in the upper regions.

Pictures and flashcards of recent and new vocabulary items can be fixed to the ceiling with blu-tack, or pinned if there is a polystyrene covering. If the class is at the copy-writing stage, then sentence cards with the week or fortnight's material can be attached to the ceiling as a memory-aid for the more able and a life-line for the less endowed.

Plus ça change! A sound reason for the division of the room into rational areas is the need for the regular variation and change of display. If we know and can see clearly what each area is, then this will help us considerably to *a* see when a display area needs changing, and *b* work and concentrate on a specific area without disrupting the rest.

As far as the time available to the teacher is concerned, we are all familiar with those situations, some foreseeable but many not, when the time for lessons, not to mention classroom decoration, is whisked away from us. So once more we return to the children. They must be involved in the redecoration.

Apart from relying on the children for much of the actual classroom decoration, one has to assume that it will be they who produce many of the source materials for displays. It will be they who bring in the cereal boxes for stiff card, the magazines and mail-order catalogues from which to find the visuals, the tickets, match-boxes, food cartons and labels from their or friends' and relations' visits to France, Belgium, Luxembourg and Canada.

If the teacher starts by giving the class a brief idea of what display areas it is intended to produce, he will find that for some things the children will provide much of the inspiration for him. Alternatively, when they bring in individual items which they thought might just be useful, he may be able to see an immediate use for them. The teacher cannot and should not take everything upon his shoulders. If the children share the pleasure and responsibility of looking after their own room, then a process will have been started by which the French lesson becomes more vital and meaningful, simply because it is a lesson in which some of their ideas and much of their handwork has been built upon.

Activity Areas and Interest Corners

Depending on the size of the classroom, the optimum number of areas into which it divides should range between six and ten. Clearly, with the exception of the *coin géographique*, *coin des structures* and, perhaps, the *coin de vocabulaire*, the corners chosen will vary considerably from class to class and school to school, according to the interests and needs of teacher and pupil and to the materials available. The areas or corners most commonly chosen are the three mentioned above, plus the general interest corner, the object corner, the post-card corner, the photograph corner, the shop corner, the topic corner, the model corner, the graph corner, corners for the children's own material and work displays, and the comparative articles and prices corner. Normally, if the width of each individual display area is taken to be approximately six feet, then six feet times the height of the room, plus, possibly, a little ceiling space and/or a table-surface in front will give ample space to develop each individual theme.

The descriptions below give some idea as to the ways in which each corner tends to be used. They are not prescriptive, but should help with basic points and problems.

The Geography Corner (Le coin géographique)

This corner, in some guise or other, is the most commonly used display area. Teachers tend to find that the best position for it is near the door, if, as is so often the case, the latter is situated near the front of the class. The display position near the door is a strong one, as all the children have to pass it several times a day and are likely to retain some impressions of the materials on show. Additionally, many teachers like to use a map of France quite often and the logic of mounting it on the wall in a display near the front of the class is self-evident.

The geography corner may simply be a relatively large size map of France, but much may be done to exploit this basic item in a variety of ways. Assuming the provision of a straight-forward large-scale paper map (and not the flannel or felt kind which are more flexible), then a start can be made by making the labelling effective. The names of a few principal towns could simply be written out on some pieces of card and stuck as near as possible to the places on the map with the aid of some blu-tac. Much neater and more visually pleasing is the use of cardboard arrows, or a personal preference, map pins and coloured wools. Taking the first alternative, a map will look immediately more arresting if several different designs of arrows cut from white or different colour card are used as feature locators.

Let us assume that we wish to highlight towns, rivers and mountains, or surrounding countries on our map. Then, if a different colour or shape of arrow is taken for each type of feature, the map will become much clearer for the children, not just much prettier. The arrows lead back to the name-cards situated outside the main area of the map, where, again, they are immediately clearer. The easiest arrow-shapes available apart from the straight arrow are:

The Swallow-tail   The Down-tail   The Up-tail

Fig. 50

If cutting these different shape arrows is found difficult, or there is no child available to do them, then assuming also that there is no coloured card available, a quite effective form of coding can be achieved by merely colouring the arrow-tips.

The same job can be done by map pins and coloured wools, with a saving on time. One may use the same colour wool and pins, i.e. green to green, blue to blue, brown to brown, as this looks much neater than different colour wools with different colour pins.

Once the children have achieved a basic familiarity with the towns, rivers, mountains, etc., on the map, games such as 'Look for the Mistake' (*Cherchez l'Erreur!*), 'Odd Man Out' (*Cherchez l'Intrus!*), 'Kim's Game' can be developed.

Cherchez l'Erreur! can be varied by the device of a single mistake within a grouping, e.g. slipping *Le Rhône* into a series of mountain-ranges, or putting four or five towns etc. in the right place and getting one wrongly placed, but within the correct classification.

Cherchez l'Intrus! will clearly be a similar activity to the first, which can be varied by our producing a town or river that we have not looked at before or a single feature outside of France, e.g. *Londres* in amongst five French towns or amongst a mixture of French rivers, mountains and towns.

Wool arrows have a particular advantage when one comes to use the map for number, distance and kilometre work. If, for instance, the teacher devises a short activity along the lines of *À Quelle Distance de Paris se trouve ... ?*, then these arrows make it much easier to see the relative distances. To give extra clarity to the exercise, a metre rule can be placed on the teacher's or another front desk and the various arrows removed and pinned into the desk, in line with the rule. Distances can then be read off quite easily according to the scale and the rule. Such an activity will be relevant even to third year secondary school level where it can be used for practising larger numbers and the structures *plus (loin, près) que ... moins (loin, près) que ....*, but it can also be used in a simplified form for number work on simple hundreds lower down the age group, as long as the towns are carefully chosen. For those who are keen on extending the scope of French outside the French lesson, such an activity can well be adapted to the maths lesson.

Another effective device for use with the map as a basis is the arrowed photograph or magazine or brochure picture, acting as a substitute for the name-card on a map display. Apart from looking very pleasing, a circle of smallish pictures framing or lying inside the map can do much to fix places and their significance in the mind of the child in a way in which ordinary name-cards never can, particularly, of course, if they are arrowed on to their target rather than stuck near to the place they are supposed to represent without any precise location. Without definition, a picture of the Pont du Gard stuck on a map could just as easily be Nîmes, Arles or Orange to the average pupil.

Even with a large wall map, there is the temptation to fill it and its borders too full of pictures, because a plentiful supply happens to be available. Always in display, clutter is a major trap and a major enemy. Too much is as bad as too little and overloading can spoil a display that promised well. If there is an abundance of material, the best strategy is to use it gradually, not only to prevent the pupil from having to penetrate through a maze of material to see what he or she wants or is supposed to see, but also because material presentation spread over a period is also spread effort.

A small point, but one that has an important effect on the efficiency of the map display is the actual size of the map in relation to its display area. The various non-map activities outlined below make it essential that it does not fill the whole of the wall area allocated to the *coin géographique* if the display area is to obtain its maximum effect. Apart from the fact that with regard to the map itself there must be a free area outside of it for the arrowed photographs and pictures discussed above, there are such things as separate photo and picture displays, regional, souvenir, commercial products, local industry and food displays which need wall space as well as a table surface to complete the L-shape.

The photo/picture display, which is a logical extension of the arrowed map illustrations discussed above, is flexible and lends itself to easy partial or total change. Though it could be accommodated on the table surface, its natural habitat is the wall.

Photographs and pictures can be grouped much more satisfyingly on the wall because of the greater space available. Daylight left between pictures can do much to help the eye. Though it can make a pleasant change (and a good revision session!) to have a random display of vaguely geographic pictures up on the wall, most colleagues will normally prefer thematic grouping, both from the point of view of short or long-term planning and the child's meaningful learning.

Small displays can be initiated on houses (and regional styles), dress, transport, regional peculiarities, a specific region, local industries, delicacies, dishes, beverages, battle towns, famous historical cities, twinned towns, fishing ports, naval ports, castles, cathedrals, inter alia.

The Grammar Corner (Coin des Structures)

Many teachers find this particular *coin* essential as a provider of visual reinforcement of the new work attempted in the current units or chapters of the commercial courses with which they are working. It is at its most effective, of course, if it is designed with the additional flexibility to allow it to be used within the lesson when required. Here one notes the justification for the L-shaped corner. Pictures and sentence-cards can be difficult to take down from the wall to use in a hurry and can be quite time-consuming even when we have the luxury of a little time to get the class-room set-up. The table surface, with its easily usable realien and perhaps a few not so solidly attached wall-pieces can provide a basis for easy lesson use.

A teacher with a first year French class may well decide, at least for the first few months, to have no written reinforcement for his visual material. The introduction of reading and writing is a vexed point discussed on pages 39–50, but assuming a situation where in the very earliest stages next to nothing written will be pinned and stuck to the wall, useful reinforcement for grammatical points and structures can be provided by attaching pictures, posters or figurines to the wall in some sort of logical sequence. If the course in use is one where the early work is poster-based, then it will be a straightforward matter to display unit posters in their natural order of presentation. However, in the case of a figurine-based early course, the figurines themselves must be displayed. Leaving aside for a moment the difficulties of conveying exactly the right impression from a few pieces of felt or card stuck on the wall, one meets the immediate objection that the school has at a maximum one set of figurines for each teacher and more likely something like one set between two teachers. Figurines are still relatively cheap teaching materials and, over a period of two or three years, it should be possible to order enough sets to have one for each teacher of French and at least one spare set. At all events, figurines do wear out, as we know, and do need to be replaced.

Those which are no longer fit for frequent handling in front of the class can, with some judicious trimming and repair, offer valuable service on the wall. Should neither additional new sets nor partly worn-out ones be available, then excellent substitutes, often more attractive than the original, can be made by children tracing over the outline on to hard card and colouring them in.

Let us now examine the situation where we already have our figurines and are preparing to display them on our wall surface. If it is remembered also that the very initial stages of the children's encounter with French are being discussed and there may very well be no written word on the wall apart from the corner headings, then one is confronted by a problem which most colleagues will have met at some time or other. How do you convey meaning accurately by picture only? Before discussing individual examples, a majority of teachers will agree that certain structures and ideas are very difficult to display pictorially on a flat surface, due partly to the difficulties of attachment and partly to the problems created by a change from a three-dimensional to a two-dimensional medium. For example, *Jeannot est derrière l'arbre* is easy enough to demonstrate to the class using one's hands and moving the figurines to show the spatial relationship, but a figurine of a tree placed on top of *Jeannot* and then pinned to the wall loses the concept of 'behind' for many people. If, however, the teacher makes his own magazine-picture figurines to supplement the commercially produced figurines, then pictures can be selected to overcome such spatial and semantic difficulties. Almost any magazine would provide at least one picture to transmit the idea of 'behind' clearly.

As so much of the early grammar or structure work is concerned with elementary questions and their answers, *Qu'est-ce que c'est?* ... *Qui est-ce?* ... *Où va-t-il?*, coded question marks can be used to surmount the problem of the lack of a written cue in wall displays. As their name implies, coded question marks are merely question marks made from card and given a standardised colour-coding. If for example a green question-mark is held up during the early stages of asking *Qu'est-ce que c'est?*, and similarly a yellow one when dealing with *Qui est-ce?*, then coded question marks soon come to have considerable meaning for the pupils.

An example of a successful early and related activity is the *Qu'est-ce que c'est?/Qui est-ce?* mime, where a child, in front of the class or in his or her group, mimes an object or person and holds up the green or yellow question mark, eliciting both question and answer from the audience. Such an activity is a useful revision device as it allows practice in several different structures (including the responses) and obliges the children to put the question.

The *où* coded question mark is particularly helpful in the early stages, both from the point of view of pupil participation in the questioning and from that of maintaining impetus during question and answer sessions.

But, additionally, direction-arrows can be used when dealing with early reinforcement of *où*. Thus, a short sequence of a figurine of a boy+direction-arrow+the *où* question mark, with a church some distance away, the whole sequence leading from left to right, produces: *Paul, où va-t-il? ... Il va à l'église.*

With early beginners, the table surface can serve the useful purpose of complementing the wall picture-structures in the most straightforward of ways. Assuming realien for the table are chosen to represent the concrete objects that figure in the unit of work, then the children and the teacher are afforded the opportunity to set up and practise the situations they have been dealing with. To take again the example, *où va-t-il/elle?*, if a few person-figurines are set out on the table plus a small model church, station, farm-house or all-purpose building on to which an appropriate label is simply stuck (pharmacie, cinéma, etc.), then the structure can be exploited by the use of different persons and buildings. Such a basic activity can be used for cementing basic logical connections, e.g. by holding up both *le fermier* and *la ferme* or *le facteur* and *la poste*, *le pharmacien* and *la pharmacie*. This particular activity, although so simple is especially useful, because it allows the children to see relationships between words, both in an environmental sense—*le facteur* and *la poste*—and in a linguistic context—*le pharmacien* and *la pharmacie*.

One should, however, be careful not to overdo such activities as logical relationships, since it may become habit for the child to associate particular pairs of items all the time. Over-practice of *Le fermier, où va-t-il? ... Il va à la ferme* is likely to result in a semi-permanent response of *à la ferme* to *whatever* building/place stimulus is employed. However, if such logical relationships are practised reasonably frequently in the early stages with beginners and the need for variation remembered, then very useful associations can be made by the child.

Assuming one adopts a methodical approach of sufficient spoken practice before the written material is displayed, what is going to be produced in the way of things written? There is an obvious need for labelling in the geography and the vocabulary corners and, at some time or other, in all of the other corners one devises. But, what else is there besides what might be termed naming labels and sentence cards for what is new or just old in the *coin des structures*?

Let us start with sentence cards and see what develops.

In the very early stages, a beginning can be made by writing on hard card the ordinary sentences that occur in the chapter or unit of the course and using them to reinforce the picture equations suggested above on this page. If there are posters forming something of a narrative sequence, a poster display with the relevant sentence cards underneath can be put up to produce a little story in words and pictures, a more sophisticated version of the *Rupert Bear* format. If the course supplies posters and matching sentence cards, such a display is already there, in essence.

Children seem to be rather partial to this kind of display, as they find it resembles their comics.

Sentence cards do not have to be a rectangular piece of card two inches by two feet. They will very often be this, as such a format fits in well with most display and classroom demonstration purposes, but for a change let them be a balloon.

Balloon sentences are usually a considerable success, partly because the children think it is marvellous to have a comic on the wall, and partly because the balloon shape provides interest and direction for the eye and a welcome change from everything being written in square sentences. For these reasons, apart from their use in reinforcing language, they add a brightness to the room, and once again the feeling that something is going on. Comic wall-displays of this type are especially suitable for activities like 'Fill in the Blanks!' (*Remplissez les Blancs!*) and are extremely easy to set up. The class shut their eyes while the teacher or a pupil removes one balloon sentence (or more) and then puts the question/statement *Qu'est-ce qui manque? Remplissez le Blanc!*

The balloon concept also helps to reinforce structure picture-sentences. While ordinary sentence cards underneath a picture-sentence or picture-sentence sequence such as:

Où vas-tu, Paul? ... Je vais à la boulangerie.

or

Combien de vélos y a-t-il? ... Il y en a douze.

reinforce in a perfectly adequate manner, it is interesting to note how a balloon sentence placed near the mouth of each speaker makes the point even clearer because the class can see who is saying what.

Colour-coding is a particular boon when it comes to helping the less able groups to do something for themselves. For example, sentences relating to individual pictures or picture-displays can be written on different colour card and grouped randomly at the bottom of the display. To focus the pupils' attention in the right direction, picture and sentence can be correctly linked by the simple device of a square of the right coloured card being placed next to the visual. e.g. if the sentence *L'aéroport est à 10 kilomètres de Toulouse* is printed on pink card, then a small square of pink card will be placed next to the visuals representing that sentence.

Split sentences, requiring somewhat more input on the part of the beginner or less able child, also combine help for the pupil with at least a small element of challenge. They are merely straightforward sentences culled from current work, printed on card and cut somewhere near the middle in a fairly distinctive manner, so that the child can be guided by the cut (see Fig. 18).

Jig-saw sentences are simply an extension of split sentences and, like the latter, can be displayed randomly on the wall or table and left for the children to fit together as part of a lesson or group activity. They are another material containing a fun element and it is interesting to note how the casual eye, having scanned an incomplete sentence will search for its completion on the wall, when it will often glide past the completed utterance.

The Vocabulary Corner
The *coin de vocabulaire* is perhaps the easiest corner to set up and maintain. At its most basic, it is just an area of wall (or an L-shape) to which are attached visuals of the new vocabulary encountered. It serves, of course, as a reminder of the new words involved, during the week or fortnight on the new material. If, however, there is a need to make the corner more effective, other things can be done in addition to attaching new visuals to the wall. One might divide the display space into sections—*a* new unit vocabulary *b* new incidental vocabulary and *c* revision vocabulary, probably giving pride of place to *a*. Within each section, the effectiveness may be increased by grouping the vocabulary according to gender in two columns, the one topped by *un* done in blue letters, the other by *une* in pink.

Sections *a* and *c* are self-explanatory, but the section for new incidental vocabulary requires some discussion.

Teachers tend to be wary of introducing into their lesson any vocabulary which is not to be found in the Teacher's Book. This reluctance has occurred, of course, partly because many currently available commercial materials seem to assume a rate of progress so rapid as to be impossible to maintain if anything not already there is added to the lesson. At the primary and middle-school levels, there has also been the anxiety of knowing that much is expected by the receiver school to which one's children will depart. The syllabus must be covered. This is all too understandable, but, there is room for extraneous vocabulary; especially if the children come up and want to know what things are—things that have not been catered for by the course book. One can keep faith with one's syllabus and time-schedule by incorporating such outside, child-requested vocabulary in the examples used to reinforce new language points and in the simpler, more relevant dialogues sometimes invented to supplement and, perhaps, replace those found in the book. For example there is no reason why, when the children are being familiarised with means of transport and the structures used, teacher and pupils should not be able to substitute

> *Jules y va en tracteur/hydroglisseur/hélicoptère/fusée.*

for

> *Jules y va en voiture.*

Colour, interest and meaning all help the mind to remember. Constant refusal to give simple vocabulary for the things our pupils want to know about leads to sheer frustration, and there is evidence to suggest that continual frustration of such attempts to learn leads to negative reactions to French on the part of the pupil. They begin to dislike it, because they seem to be stopped from learning when they want to and feel the need to know.

A final justification for the inclusion of additional vocabulary is the peculiar vertical nature of so much course material. Let us look at the supplementary transport vocabulary again. If the children are introduced to various means of transport, it is a peculiar and disturbing situation for them when they seem to be given vehicles which are chosen quite arbitrarily while others, just as important to them, are left out. They are secure in their mother tongue, because they can talk about all the forms of transport they need to talk about. But in what ought to be a parallel situation in their second language, at least at a straightforward level, one seems sometimes to be encouraging them to talk, but not to talk. If new vocabulary from outside the course does not interfere with the structure, is not impossibly difficult to pronounce, and helps to give a child a feeling of completeness within the topic area, one should feel able to use it.

A practical difficulty is the limitation of the teacher's own French vocabulary. If a child came up to the average teacher and asked what the French for 'hovercraft' was, he would perhaps be fortunate to receive *hydroglisseur/aéroglisseur*. Nor would it necessarily be a good thing to conjure pieces of vocabulary out of the air and blow them at the pupils. New vocabulary ought not to be given in isolation, along the lines of 'What's a "hovercraft" in French?'—'*Hydroglisseur . . . un hydroglisseur*'. As far as possible, one should try to introduce it with the structures being used. But, returning to the more basic problem, how does the teacher encourage enquiry after new vocabulary and save his dignity when he does not know the word on the spot. An easy escape is to have a weekly request-list, the answers to which are supplied the week after, after that is, one has had the time to look things up.

As with so many aspects of teaching, it is a question of striking the right balance. Should one fall into the habit of introducing so much extra vocabulary that the children do not have the opportunity of becoming properly familiar with those items they are supposed to have mastered within the commercial course on which they are being reared, then one is causing problems for their future school career.

Whether or not the stage of introducing the written word has been reached, vocabulary visuals grouped on display will be justifying their position simply by being there. But one can do more than just placing the vocabulary on the wall.

Vocabulary grouping is a useful aid at the pre-written word stage.

Words which have some logical reason for being grouped together will tend to offer the early learner some opportunity for forming associations between them. Also of course, some relationship may already have been created for the words within the lesson. If the children have been working with *je* and *mange, bois, lis, dors, joue*, then the links should already have been forged and visuals of a person performing each of those actions should set off some interreaction amongst them in the minds of many of the pupils, particularly if the visuals have been grouped together.

Relation-pairings can also be effectively brought out and reinforced by simple display on the wall. If the children can see our old friend the *fermier* with his *ferme* placed next to him, or the *facteur* and *une lettre, le receveur* and *un autobus, un cycliste* and *un vélo, l'hôpital* and *une ambulance*, etc., then relationships become relatively easy to fix. Simple activities like mixing all the paired visuals and then encouraging the pupils to rearrange them in their common associative pairings will not be time wasted.

Similarly much constructive work can be done at an early stage with rhyming pairs and groups. Even at a quite advanced level rhyming vocabulary association can prove a useful means of cementing vocabulary and underlining associations. If the teacher looks for rhyming material in the early units of his commercial course, he will not find it difficult to come up with a considerable supply of visuals for the wall containing single or double-syllable rhymes and different words pronounced exactly the same, e.g.

pain   pêche   chou   bouche   bois   café
train   bêche   clou   mouche   doigt   café

épicerie   téléphone   dix   verre
charcuterie   magnétophone   vis   vert

bateau   agent   cage   frère
château   dent   page   mère
gâteau   vent   plage   père

A great number of teachers have found rhyme-work to be a salutary experience over the years, because it so often shows that it is unwise to take too many basic assumptions for granted. In the examples quoted above, it is interesting to note how many children do not grasp the relationship between *café* (= café) and *café* (= coffee) or *verre* and *vert*, until they see the items on the wall together. In contrast, it is not just the bright child who will come up and ask if *-erie* has something to do with 'shops and things'. More than most devices, rhyming-work is a continual reminder that young second-language learners do not necessarily see things and relationships uniformly or in the same way as experienced adults.

Rhyme-work and display are also useful when the teacher is tackling the early copy-writing stage, for relating sounds and their spellings, much as in the mother-tongue, vocabulary visuals on the wall, accompanied by the written-word, with the relevant part of the word highlighted in colour, will do much to cement the pattern with the pupil.

Two General Points

The Prop and Costume Store
A majority of teachers rely on children acting out structures, situations and dialogues as the basis of their method. Yet, well as this may proceed, they may often feel they are not making the most of a very rich source of activity. They are concerned when they do not help certain children overcome their embarrassment and reticence when acting in front of the class. They assume that it is the pupils' lack of command of their second language, but they are not sure. Equally, they question whether large amounts of lesson time spent with a few children acting out at the front, while the rest sit listening and not listening, is the most productive use of precious time. A gradually built-up prop and costume store can help to solve both of these different yet overlapping problems.

One asks a boy to act like a *garçon de café* and one may be lucky. He is given a waistcoat, tray and tea-towel and a little less luck is needed. The word 'prop' is well-chosen. With a few items to go with the character and create the visual stereotype, the boy or girl acting has been given a head start.

If there are enough 'clothes and things' (the children's own words), then several groups can be working at the same time and help to use the time available more productively. (See chapter on Group work.)

The Post-Box (La Bôite à Lettres)
A major classroom item, the *bôite à lettres*, is under-employed if it is only used for decoration.

When the pupils' level of French is sufficiently high for them to be writing simple letters, an obvious tactic is to post them in the class letter-box; and how much more do they gain from the process if their letters are actually answered! Such a scheme is easily devised if the class is divided into two halves, everybody is given a new French identity and children in Half *A* requested to write to those in Half *B* and vice versa. Initial and even later letter-writing along these lines would be guided and helped by civilisation material on the areas from which the children are supposed to come. The procedure can be given a touch of reality by the use of envelopes with (used) French stamps on them.

A worthwhile technique like the post-box routine ought not to have to wait for the pupil to reach the stage where he or she can actually write in French. It is justifiable as a means of eliciting creative letter-writing in English, and is most useful for cementing the background French material acquired in class.

Further Reading

BBC—Teaching Languages—Ideas and Guidance for Teachers Working with Adults. Ed. E. R. Baer. B.B.C. Publications.
M. BUCKBY & D. GRANT—Faites vos Jeux. Materials Development Unit, Language Teaching Centre, University of York.
J. DAKIN—The Language Laboratory and Language Learning. Longman.
A. W. HORNSEY Ed.—Handbook for Modern Language Teachers. Methuen Educational.
G. C. HAYTER—Using Broadcasts in Schools: a Study and Evaluation. BBC/ITV.
P. D. PUMFREY—Reading: tests and assessment techniques. Hodder and Stoughton.
B. RAPAPORT & D. WESTGATE—Children Learning French. Methuen Educational.
SCHOOLS COUNCIL—Concept 7–9. A Schools Council Curriculum Project. Arnold.
A. WRIGHT—Visual Materials for the Language Teacher. Longman.
C. WRINGE—Developments in Modern Language Teaching. Open Books.
G. VARNAVA—Mixed-Ability Teaching in Modern Languages. Blackie.

Useful Addresses

Centre for Information on Language Teaching and Research, 20, Carlton House Terrace, London, SW1Y 5AP.
The Secretary, The School Broadcasting Council, BBC, London, W1A 1AA.
Education Office, Independent Broadcasting Authority, Brampton Road, London, SW3 1EY.
British Association for Language Teaching (formerly Audio-Visual Language Association), sec. David Nott, 15, Southdown Crescent, Cheadle Hulme, Cheshire.
Modern Language Association, 24a, Highbury Grove, London, N5 2EA

Index

Achievement, certificates of 93
Alternative curriculum 92
Assessment 18
Average ability pupils 19

Captions 103
Car, the 71
Cataloguing 90
Class control 91
Classroom instructions 85
Class routine 88
Cloze activities 33
Commands 86
Commerce 74
Comprehension work 10
Concentration 23
Conversations 12
Cookery 72
Crosswords 37
CSE, Modes II and III 93

Difficult schools and children 91–93
Display 94–108
   Pupil participation 94
   Classroom division 95
   L-shaped structure 96
   The ceiling 96
   Changes 97
   Activity areas 98

Early learners 39

Fashion 73
Figurines 101
Flexible French 18

Football 75

Geography corner 98
Gist reading 40
Grammar corner 101
Group work
   Teacher control 3
   Lesson adaptation 4
   Group practice 6
   Mixed-ability 17–24
   Group cycle 21
   Oral techniques 25, 42
   Peer situations 25
   Activities 8, 25–43

Humour 78

Initiative activities 36
Interrogatives 26

Jig-saw sentences 49
Job-centred activities 72

Linguistic conventions 33
Logical relationships 107
Lower-ability pupils 23

Mixed-ability 17–24
   Independent group work 17
   Flexible French 17
   Responsibility for assessment 18
   Course adaptations 4, 51–54
Monitoring 14

Noise 15

Offset copier 80
Oral lesson (total) 15
Overhead projector 60–62, 79–80

Photographic slides 78
Photos 78
Practical activities 72, 92
Pupil participation 47, 88–91, 94

Question–Answer patterns 26

Radio broadcasts 62–67
Reading (silent) 39
Register in French 87
Re-practice 34
Role-playing 108

Seating arrangements 21–22
Sentence cards 103
Single skill testing 20
Sound recall 54
Structure practice 14
Substitution translation 50
Survival situations 93

Tape-recorder 40, 81–83
    Leader tapes 81
    Tapes—Teacher and Assistant made 82
    Microphone 82
    Sound effects 83

Signature tunes 83
    Radio programmes 84
Top ability pupils 19, 24

Visuals, preparation of 76–81
    Picture sources 76
    Adhesives 76
    Professional finish 77
    Photos 78
    Photographic slides 78
    Overhead projector 79
    Offset copier 80
    Projector prints 81
Vocabulary corner 105

Workcards 44–67
    Group work 44
    Grading 44
    Basic card 46
    Coding 46
    Longevity 46
    Pupil production 47
    Early learners 49
    Slide cards 41
    Map cards 51
    Unit adaptation cards 53
    Filmstrip cards 56
    Overhead projector cards 60
    Radio cards 62
    Exploded texts 64
    Multiple choice 65
    Language laboratory cards 67